ILLUSTRATED REGIONAL GUIDES TO

ANCIENT MONUMENTS

under the ownership or guardianship of
The Ministry of Works

Volume II

SOUTHERN ENGLAND

by

THE RT. HON. LORD HARLECH, P.C., K.G., G.C.M.G., F.S.A.,
formerly First Commissioner of Works

LONDON: HER MAJESTY'S STATIONERY OFFICE

1952

First edition 1936
Second edition 1952
Second impression with amendments 1955

CONTENTS

	PAGE
PREFACE	5
PREHISTORIC PERIOD	9
Neolithic	9
Bronze Age	11
Iron Age	18
ROMAN PERIOD	25
ANGLO-SAXON PERIOD	31
THE MIDDLE AGES	
Ecclesiastical Buildings	35
Secular Buildings	
(i) Castles	39
Norman	40
Fourteenth-Century	46
Tudor	48
(ii) Houses	50
RENAISSANCE	51
NOTES	55
BIBLIOGRAPHY	77
INDEX	79

ILLUSTRATIONS

			Between pages
Plate 1	AVEBURY	⎫	
2	TRETHEVY QUOIT	⎬ 8 and 9	
3	STONEHENGE		
4	MAIDEN CASTLE	⎭	
5	RICHBOROUGH CASTLE	⎫	
6	PORTCHESTER CASTLE	⎬ 24 and 25	
7	PEVENSEY CASTLE		
8	OLD SARUM	⎭	
9	DOVER CASTLE	⎫	
10	,, ,, UPPER CHAPEL IN KEEP	⎬ 40 and 41	
11	CARISBROOKE CASTLE		
12	RESTORMEL CASTLE	⎭	
13	NUNNEY CASTLE	⎫	
14	DARTMOUTH CASTLE	⎬ 56 and 57	
15	ST. MAWE'S CASTLE		
16	TITCHFIELD ABBEY	⎭	
17	MUCHELNEY ABBEY	⎫	
18	NETLEY ABBEY	⎬ 72 and 73	
19	OLD WARDOUR CASTLE		
20	GREENWICH, QUEEN'S HOUSE	⎭	

PREFACE TO THE FIRST EDITION

In the preface to the first volume of this series of regional guides for visitors to the Ancient Monuments under the guardianship of the Office of Works I explained the scope and object of the series. The first edition of the first volume covering the six Northern Counties of England was sold out in a few weeks, and a second edition has now been issued.

Thus encouraged, I have written this second volume of the series, covering the monuments for which the Office is responsible in the counties south of the River Thames. I hope to include the remaining English monuments in the Midlands and East Anglia in a third volume, to be prepared in the course of this year, leaving Scotland and Wales to be dealt with separately at a later date.

In addition to the list of the monuments, county by county, giving the hours of opening and cost of admission to the public, and a map showing their whereabouts, and photographs of some of the most important, I have again provided in the form of an introduction a general description of the monuments in their chronological and historical settings. This survey is designed to help the ordinary visitor to understand what he or she is looking at.

The ever-increasing number of visitors to our national monuments shows that there is a growing circle of those who take a pride and interest in such things. For the sake of these visitors not only does the Department devote increasing care to the amenity and settings of the monuments but has prepared these regional guides and more technical handbooks to each of the more important individual monuments.

This second volume covers an area that contains such outstanding prehistoric monuments as Avebury, Stonehenge, and Maiden Castle. It includes the important Roman fortresses of Richborough and Portchester, and the mediæval castles of Dover and Carisbrooke. Whereas Volume I dealt with a number of abbeys and priories, only Netley in this volume is of the same order of importance as those in our Northern Counties. This volume, however, includes a number of interesting monuments that are at present less well known than they deserve, such as the very beautiful castle of Restormel in Cornwall, the romantic Tintagel, a number of Henry VIII's coast defence castles, and the delightful Queen's House at Greenwich built by Inigo Jones.

I should like to take this opportunity of acknowledging the assistance given me by independent archæologists as well as by the staff of my own Ancient Monuments Department in the preparation of these regional guides.

W. ORMSBY-GORE.

OFFICE OF WORKS,
   April 1936.

PREFACE TO THE SECOND EDITION

This series of guides to the Ancient Monuments of Great Britain under the care of the Ministry of Works was designed by Lord Harlech, and began to be published under his inspiration when he was the Rt. Hon. W. Ormsby-Gore, M.P., and First Commissioner of Works. He himself wrote the first three volumes, on Northern, Southern and Central England, which were issued in 1935-8. The fifth volume on North Wales, also written by him, was published in 1948. During the war the earlier volumes went out of print: this new edition has been brought up to date with the author's consent by the inclusion of additional monuments taken over since 1939, and by some revision in cases where the discovery of new evidence has led to a modification of previous theories. With these exceptions, however, the text in each case remains substantially that of the original author.

DAVID ECCLES,
Minister of Works.

MINISTRY OF WORKS,
November 1951.

Plate 1. AVEBURY

Plate 2. TRETHEVY QUOIT

Plate 3. STONEHENGE

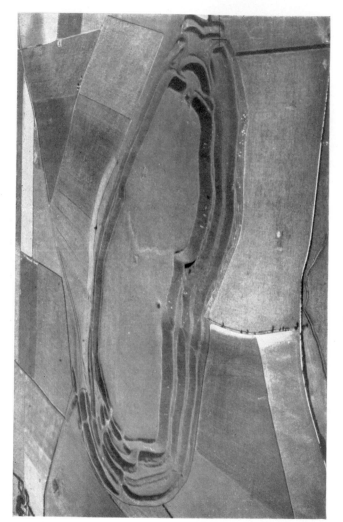

Plate 4. MAIDEN CASTLE

PREHISTORIC PERIOD

From its geographical position in relation to the Continent of Europe, the south of England naturally furnishes us with the evidence of successive influences which, either by trade or by invasion, affected the population of England from the earliest times to the Roman conquest.

As this is a guide to monuments, and not an archæological treatise, it is unnecessary to trace layer by layer the full story from the earliest evidences of human occupation in our island, such as the "eoliths", or most primitive stone implements of Kent and the Piltdown skull of Sussex, and it must suffice to begin with the period of our earliest monuments, which date from towards the end of the neolithic or Late Stone Age period about 2000 B.C.

NEOLITHIC

The arrival from more than one source of new peoples with a neolithic culture effected a profound revolution in Britain. They were the first comers to our island to own domestic animals, to cultivate the soil with grain crops, to make pottery, to grind and polish stone implements as well as to chip them, to construct defensible hill-top camps, and finally to erect monuments to their important dead in the style known as "megalithic", involving the use of huge blocks of stone. Almost any one of these "inventions" would have marked a revolution in human progress, but the evidence seems to point to the conclusion that all these great developments took place somewhere about the same time, by the convergence on Britain of several streams of migration from continental Europe. These peoples found on our chalk downs and open limestone plateaux almost ideal conditions for settlement and for the life their knowledge then enabled them to lead. And so it is mainly along our southern coasts and on the uplands of Sussex, Dorset and Wiltshire that we find evidences of our late neolithic civilization in the form of flint-mines, long barrows, and hill-top camps, of the type known as "Causeway camps" which are peculiar to this period. One such Causeway camp has recently been identified beneath the later Iron Age fortifications of *Maiden Castle* in Dorset (Plate 4), which is in our guardianship.

The archæological evidence would seem to point to three main sources of invasion. First, from Portugal and Spain, probably by way of Brittany, to our south-west coasts, particularly Cornwall, as also to Wales, Ireland, western and extreme northern Scotland. Second, from Switzerland and eastern France, where we find the continental parallels to our Causeway camps, and smooth round-bottomed pottery, now usually called "Windmill Hill" pottery, from the extensive deposits of it at *Windmill Hill* near *Avebury* in Wiltshire. Third, from the Baltic, from which was brought to England the type of pottery known as "Peterborough ware", found on the edges of the Fens but also in and near *Avebury* and elsewhere.

The simplest examples of megalithic remains are probably the Dolmens, or Cromlechs as they are sometimes erroneously called. It is difficult to prove but equally difficult to disprove that these owe their origin to the Atlantic influence from Portugal and Spain. They consist of a gigantic horizontal capstone resting on a polygonal structure of large stone uprights, similar to the Dolmens of Portugal, Brittany, Anglesey, and Denmark. Archæologists agree that of those standing free to-day, many were in fact originally the chambers of burial mounds from which the earth has been removed during the last four thousand years.

Trethevy Quoit in Cornwall (Plate 2) is a typical monument of this class in our guardianship, and another which apparently belongs to the same class is *Kit's Coty House* in Kent. *Little-Kit's Coty House* nearby is a ruined example probably of the same type, and is also in our guardianship.

Of Long Barrows containing megalithic burial chambers there are three in our guardianship in this area, namely, *Wayland's Smithy* in Berkshire, *West Kennett* near *Avebury* in Wiltshire, and *Stoney Littleton* near Wellow in Somerset. *Wayland's Smithy* is much denuded and its chambers are partly exposed. It was excavated 1919-20 and presents some features unusual in most other long barrows. *West Kennett*—one of the largest in Britain—was unfortunately excavated in the middle of the nineteenth century before the science and art of archæology had made the progress they have of recent years; like *Wayland's Smithy* it is much denuded, and the megalithic termination at its eastern end is now partly exposed. In it were found numbers of broken human bones, and fragments of Peterborough and Beaker ware. *Stoney Littleton* was also excavated in the nineteenth century, and was then comprehensively restored before being handed over to our guardianship in 1884. Its covering of earth and its chambers are largely intact, and it presents a very perfect picture of the internal structure of a long barrow.

It is generally thought that the long barrows with terminal chambers are the earliest, and that those with side chambers and a "false door" are later, and that the "passage graves" are later still. But one of the most frequent causes of archæological uncertainty is the common re-use of barrows for secondary burials in later ages. Barrows, like our modern churchyards, were often used as sacred repositories for the remains of the dead by successive generations from neolithic to Saxon times, and it is sometimes difficult to be sure from the finds in them that the original or primary use has been identified.

Our long barrow people seem to have been everywhere predominantly dolichocephalic or long-skulled, and thus to be clearly demarcated from the next large-scale invasion of a new people from Germany in the early years of the second millenium B.C. The latter were predominantly brachycephalic or roundheaded, and buried their dead in a crouching position. These new invaders are known as the "Beaker Folk", from their characteristic fine decorated pottery. During the few centuries in which they were dominant the earliest bronze tools and weapons were introduced by trade, and the Beaker folk are usually included in the Early Bronze Age in Britain.

BRONZE AGE

There can be little doubt that the Beaker people first landed on the southern and eastern coasts of Britain and gradually spread to and occupied other parts of the country. Finds of actual beakers would seem to show that the occupation was more intensive in certain clearly defined areas: (1) The Yorkshire Wolds. (2) The Peak district of Derbyshire. (3) Wiltshire and Dorset. (4) The eastern edges of the Fens and parts of the East Anglian coast. (5) The Thames estuary and valley. (6) Northumberland. (7) Aberdeenshire and Kincardineshire.

In Wessex, at the end of the Beaker period, the arrival of rich warriors from Brittany opened up extensive trade relations, which brought amber from the Baltic, gold and bronze from

Ireland, and blue faïence beads from as far away as Egypt. The members of the new aristocracy were buried in a distinctive form of round barrow, the bell barrow, which has a conical mound and a carefully made ditch encircling it, leaving a flat area or berm between the two. For the first time cremation became the dominant rite.

It may be advisable in this connection to recall that the Icknield Way is a prehistoric track the use of which almost certainly dates back to early neolithic times. It connected the area of intensive neolithic occupation round Thetford, Brandon, and *Grime's Graves* in the Brecklands of the Little Ouse basin on the borders of Norfolk and Suffolk with the other intensively occupied area round *Avebury*. It followed the contours of the great chalk escarpment, passed Newmarket, Royston, Dunstable, Ivinghoe, Watlington, crossing the Thames at Goring, and the Berkshire downs. It runs for the most part below and north-west of the ridge, but above the spring level. All along this famous way we find evidences of neolithic man. There can be little doubt that the Beaker folk who landed from Holland on our eastern coasts penetrated to Wiltshire along this already established route.

It now looks as if we can attribute the initiation of our most remarkable prehistoric remains, namely, the megalithic stone circles, to the impact of the Beaker folk on the neolithic population with whom they mingled. Everything seems to point to the great "temple" at *Avebury* and its avenues being the achievement of the Beaker folk of the district—and if *Avebury*, then also probably *Stanton Drew* in Somerset, the earliest parts of *Stonehenge,* and other stone and wood circles in the southern counties and elsewhere in Britain.

The distribution of the megalithic stone circles of Britain is, however, curious. In areas of known Beaker folk influence we find them in Wiltshire, Somerset and Dorset, in Derbyshire, Cumberland, Aberdeenshire, and Kincardineshire. Their absence in the dense concentration of Beaker population in the Yorkshire Wolds and in East Anglia is probably to be explained simply by the lack of stone in these districts. One monument of a similar character where timber was used in place of stone has been found and excavated near Norwich, and it is probable that others await discovery, the perishable nature of timber having made their disappearance complete. On the other hand, we find megalithic circles in areas where Beaker influence is either unknown or very sparse, such as the Orkneys, the Outer Hebrides (Lewis), south-west Wales and, in the southern counties, Cornwall.

The development of Cornwall seems to have followed rather different lines from those of the rest of the district under consideration. No Causeway camps have yet been identified in the Duchy, and though the typical neolithic long barrow is found, and dolmens such as *Trethevy Quoit,* the characteristic early sepulchres of Cornwall dating from the late neolithic or earliest Bronze Age are the chambered barrows and passage graves of types found mainly in Portugal, Brittany, Wales, and Ireland. The Scilly Isles have no less than forty-three chambered barrows as against fifteen in Cornwall, mostly at its extreme western end, pointing to the use of the islands as an important maritime trade centre during the second millenium B.C. Three of the best of the tombs of Scilly are in the guardianship of the Ministry, *Bants Carn, Porth Hellick Down* and *Innisigden.*

The Beaker folk reached Cornwall only in small numbers; its cultural connections seem to have been with countries accessible by sea rather than with those reached overland. This separation is especially obvious in the case of pottery. In the Early Bronze Age the typical Cornish pottery consists of small bi-conical vessels decorated with cord impressions and having usually two handles or lugs. Early Bronze Age types common to most of the rest of Britain are unknown in Cornwall, and these Cornish vessels are hardly ever found in England outside Devon and Cornwall though they are found in Brittany and Ireland. A further connection by trade between the Land's End peninsula and Ireland is attested by the finding at Harlyn Bay of two typical Irish Early Bronze Age gold lunulæ, or crescent-shaped collars. Large numbers of these lunulæ have been found in Ireland itself, and others widely scattered in England and Scotland, one in North Wales and a few on the Continent (Denmark, Belgium, Brittany, and Spain). Everything points to their being of Irish manufacture of Early Bronze Age date, *i.e.*, about 1500 B.C. Ireland was then one of the principal sources of gold known to the prehistoric world, but Irish gold seems to have been worked out by the Early Iron Age, and was unknown in Roman times.

But in spite of these differences Cornwall has a considerable number of megalithic circles. There are at least sixteen known in the Duchy, seven concentrated in the extreme west, and nine in a fairly compact group in the region of Bodmin Moor.

The conclusion which one is inclined to draw from the available, but still scanty, data is that the megalithic "idea" was introduced to our shores by maritime adventurers from the Mediterranean *via* Portugal and Brittany, and perhaps *via* Cornwall, but that it required the political capacity and organizing power of the Beaker folk to translate this "idea" into such major works as the great stone circles and accompanying monuments of *Avebury, Stonehenge*, and *Stanton Drew*. The great Megalithic Age can be put round about 1750 B.C., but it seems likely that the idea continued in less ambitious form long after the influence of the Beaker occupation, and the veneration which such mighty remains must have inspired in subsequent generations of prehistoric man in Britain may have led to imitation on a smaller scale throughout the Bronze Age.

The greatest of all stone circles is *Avebury* (Plate 1), which was placed under the guardianship of the Ministry of Works by the National Trust. Its circle of very large blocks of sarsen contained two other smaller circles, and was surrounded by a huge bank and a fosse or ditch 50 feet deep. The modern village is mostly within the great circle, and the breaking up of the megaliths for building purposes in the eighteenth and nineteenth centuries has done much to diminish the spectacular appearance of the monument. But it is the largest prehistoric circle and fosse in the world, and enough is still visible to justify the dictum of Stukeley, the eighteenth century antiquary, that "Avebury is to Stonehenge as a cathedral is to a parish church". The *Avebury* area is without doubt the most important prehistoric site in Britain.

From the main circle an avenue of stones led south-eastwards towards the village of West Kennett. The northern end of this avenue has been systematically excavated and any stones found have been re-erected in their former positions, and the sites of the missing stones have been determined and marked, with the result that enough can now be seen to give a very fair impression of its original appearance. The avenue terminated on Overton Hill in a small circle known as the *Sanctuary*, which is in our guardianship. This consisted of two concentric circles of stones and six of timber uprights. The circles have now disappeared, but the sites of the stones and of the timbers are clearly marked.

Recently Prof. Piggott has reconsidered the plan of the *Sanctuary* and suggested that it was a roofed structure built in four phases. Originally perhaps there was only a small round hut possibly sacred in nature with a conical roof. In the next phase a circular roofed building open at the centre, seems to have been built to enclose the hut. In the third phase the earlier structures were cleared away, and replaced by what may have been a large roofed temple, with standing stones between the posts of an inner colonnade, and an entrance towards *Avebury*. In the final phase a large outer circle of stones was erected, and these were joined to the end of the West Kennett Avenue.

About a mile and a half west of the *Sanctuary* beside the main Bath road stands *Silbury Hill,* also in our guardianship. It is the largest circular artificial mound in Europe, and may possibly be connected in date and in purpose with *Avebury*, though the results of such excavations as have been made at various times are inconclusive. About half a mile to the south is the great *West Kennett* long barrow already mentioned.

Windmill Hill lies about a mile and a half to the north-west of *Avebury*. It is a prehistoric occupation site of the greatest importance, consisting of a large Causeway camp of neolithic type. Recent excavations of portions of this site have yielded immense numbers of finds of pottery of successive types, flint and stone implements, and bone artefacts of various kinds. Everything points to a large occupation, and the stratification of the deposits from the Neolithic at the bottom to the Beaker period at the top is of the utmost value to British archæology of this early period.

The whole Avebury group affords the most remarkable evidence of the height of civilization attained by the Beaker folk. These mighty works must, with the means at their command, have involved a labour and organizing ability and an intensity of purpose of a most exceptional kind. *Silbury Hill* alone must have involved the work of hundreds of men for a long time, seeing that the hard chalk had to be loosened with picks made of stone or of the antlers of the red deer, and either carried in baskets or shovelled up with implements formed from the shoulder blade-bones of animals. The digging of the great fosse at *Avebury* itself must have been a task far bigger than the dragging of the large sarsen monoliths in hundreds from the neighbouring downs, and erecting them with no little mathematical precision. That the purpose was religious there can be little doubt.

If *Avebury* is the greatest, *Stonehenge* (Plate 3) is undoubtedly the most famous of British stone circles. It is now the property of the Ministry of Works. In spite of all the study that has been devoted to it it still remains our greatest archæological mystery.* Its sophistication when compared with all other stone circles, the presence of the "blue" stones, brought almost certainly by sea all the way from Prescelly in Pembrokeshire (another centre of megalithic activity), the unique trilithons with their mortice and tenon joints, and many other features make *Stonehenge* a monument, though small in scale compared with the *Avebury* complex, that excites the wonder and speculation of scientist and amateur alike. Just as *Avebury* is but the centre of a great variety of other important prehistoric remains, so *Stonehenge* is surrounded with the traces of avenues and innumerable barrows long and round. *Avebury* and *Stonehenge* make Wiltshire the most important prehistoric county in England. In Wiltshire we have the remains or records of no less than eighty long and 2,000 round barrows, as well as early prehistoric camps, flint mines, etc., in numbers and interest such as no other area can rival.

Some two miles north-east of *Stonehenge* is another circle in our guardianship known as *Woodhenge*, near Durrington. It was discovered as a result of an air-photograph taken in 1925, and on excavation it was found to consist of a nearly circular bank with a ditch on the inside surrounding a series of six concentric circles of timber uprights. The timbers have disappeared, but their positions are marked as at the *Sanctuary*. In the area of the central ring was found the crouched skeleton of a child whose skull had been cleft through before burial—probably a dedicatory sacrifice. The pottery discovered on the site includes Beaker and other Early Bronze Age wares.

Woodhenge like the *Sanctuary*, was perhaps also a roofed structure, but in the form of a circular gallery with ridged roof, the whole open in the centre. The central area would serve for the performance of ceremonies and rites, with the spectators seated on the roof around. This reconstruction envisages a

---

* It should not be necessary to emphasize that neither *Stonehenge* nor any other stone circle had originally the smallest connection with the Druids, whose cult was not introduced into Britain till most of the stone circles were a thousand years old.

building similar to the Elizabethan theatres such as the Globe at Southwark.

Another complex of megalithic stone circles and avenues is at *Stanton Drew* in Somerset. This, and the adjacent structure known as the *Cove* are in our guardianship. There are three circles, the largest of which probably originally consisted of thirty stones, twenty-seven of which remain, but only three are still standing; the smallest was of eight stones, seven of which are still upright; and the third was originally of twelve stones, all of which are fallen. The two former circles are approached by converging avenues. There is no record of any excavation ever undertaken at *Stanton Drew*, which of all stone circles bears the most striking analogies with *Avebury*, and will doubtless repay the effort of really scientific exploration.

Two other stone circles in our guardianship are one at *Kingston Russell* and the small one known as the *Nine Stones* at Winterborne Abbas. Both are in Dorset between Dorchester and Bridport. Of Cornish examples *"The Hurlers"* near St. Cleer, which is now in our guardianship, consists of three large circles in a line near together. Close to them is a large round barrow in which was found a skeleton burial with a very early bronze dagger, and a small gold drinking cup which is now in the British Museum.

After the great outpouring of effort in the Late Neolithic-Early Bronze Age overlap, which saw the invasion of so many newcomers from distant lands, the Bronze Age in England seems to have settled down to a millenium of local evolution without further large-scale movement of peoples. Trade with Ireland for gold, and with the Baltic for amber went on, but no great invasion occurred, and consequently there was independent development of pottery and bronze types.

But about 1,000 years after the invasion of the Beaker folk we are presented, especially in the southern counties, in the Late Bronze Age with the widespread evidence of the appearance of a culture, ultimately, from Central Europe, which is often called the Urnfield culture, from the extensive cemeteries of cremation burials in urns set in flat graves, from which the greatest knowledge of this culture has been derived. In England it only made its appearance gradually, and its influence was mostly felt in Sussex, Hampshire, Dorset and Wiltshire. In this country it is often referred to as the Deverel-Rimbury culture, from the urnfields found in western Wiltshire and Dorset.

It was probably in the epoch of the late Bronze Age that Cornish tin began to be worked on anything approaching a large scale for trade overseas, and such workings are associated with remains closely akin to those of the Deverel-Rimbury culture; but there is evidence of tin having been worked before this time, and much of the bronze used in England, at least in the latter part of the Bronze Age, must have been made with Cornish tin.

Our knowledge of the Bronze Age is mainly drawn from the round barrow burials which are so frequent on the open uplands of southern England, and especially obvious to-day on Salisbury Plain. But for permanent habitation the uplands seem to have been partially forsaken in many parts of England. The Causeway camps of an earlier period were no longer occupied, and the few traces of habitation found suggest a pastoral people of nomadic or semi-nomadic habits, whose cattle-enclosures are found in Cranborne Chase and on the Marlborough Downs. On Dartmoor, however, many villages of this period have been found, consisting of groups of stone-built huts with small cultivated plots, which prove an occupation of this upland region denser than at any later age.

These conditions were doubtless favoured by the warm dry climate of the Bronze Age, and it was a further climatic change to damper conditions which induced the very different habits of the succeeding age.

IRON AGE

When exactly the first iron implements came to Britain is difficult to determine, probably about 500 B.C. From about this date until the expansion of the Roman Empire the dominating fact of Central Europe was the rise in power and the widespread movements of the Celtic tribes. Archæologists have divided this long period of Celtic expansion into two main culture divisions known as Hallstatt and La Tène. The former takes its name from a great necropolis in Austria, the latter from a celebrated archæological site on the lake of Neuchâtel in Switzerland. La Tène rises to prominence as Hallstatt declines. In both we find the evolution of new types of pottery, of new weapons and implements of both bronze and iron, and ultimately of Celtic art and decoration which seems to owe motives, stylized in a characteristically Celtic way, to Ancient Greece.

In this country the Iron Age has been divided into three main periods, which for simplicity are known as A, B, and C. It will be convenient to follow this division.

A. Some time in the seventh century B.C. there began on the continent of Europe a great expansion of Celtic tribes caused by pressure from Germanic peoples moving south from the region of the Baltic. At the main point of contact, in the district of the lower Rhine, a mixed Celto-Germanic people resulted, who in later times were known as the Belgæ, and had an enormous influence on the history of Britain: but the main and immediate result of the Germanic pressure was a widespread movement of Celtic peoples during the sixth and fifth centuries B.C.

It was just at the time of this movement that the culture of La Tène was beginning to supersede that of Hallstatt, and the westward expansion of the Celts brought it into France, where it became firmly established. But this expansion also meant that those groups on the edges of the Celtic lands, who were still in the Hallstatt period of culture, were forced further out by pressure behind them, and spread to Italy, Spain, and Britain.

Thus somewhere about 500-450 B.C. there began the immigration into Britain of fairly numerous and considerable groups of people, of both sexes, of the late Hallstatt period of culture, predominantly Celtic in blood, who established the Iron Age civilization all over south-eastern England from Weymouth to the Wash, and on the coast of Yorkshire. The majority of these invaders probably came from the Rhineland and the Netherlands, but included others from the valley of the Marne. Doubtless Celtic infiltration into Britain had begun before 500 B.C., but the beginning of the Iron Age in England comes with the invaders of the fourth century B.C.

Under these invaders there was a return to permanent habitation on the uplands, and instead of a pastoral nomadic people, a settled agricultural population is attested by the widespread discovery, largely by means of aerial photography, of the Celtic field system of cultivation in terraces, known as lynchets. On the downs they built, often on the sites of the ancient neolithic Causeway camps such as Cissbury and the Trundle in Sussex, great hill-top fortresses defended by new and more formidable ramparts. The number and size of these hill-top fortress camps in Wiltshire and Dorset is very remarkable. That they were the strongholds of tribal groups seems probable, and this seems to point to a phase of tribal consolidation and consequent war-like activity and defensive needs of which there are no signs in the preceding Bronze Age. The construction, and often the enlargement, of these camps continued through the centuries preceding the Roman invasion.

In the southern region three of these early Iron Age camps are in the guardianship of the Ministry of Works, namely, *Maiden Castle,* Dorset; *Bratton Camp,* Westbury, Wiltshire, and *Uffington Castle,* Berkshire. Close to this last is the famous *White Horse,* which will be referred to again below.

B. West of the long line of Dorset and Wiltshire Iron Age A camps we enter the area of the quite different Celtic culture known as Iron Age B. The invasion which produced this culture may perhaps be connected with the exploitation of the tin mines of Cornwall, and probably belongs mainly to the first century B.C. Its effects were first felt perhaps earlier than this century in Cornwall, and it spread to Devon and Somerset (whence it influenced the A culture of Wessex and even Sussex), and also gradually permeated the Severn Valley and the Midlands. In its early stages this invasion seems once again to point to Atlantic contacts and in the main it appears that the newcomers came from Brittany, where they had close cultural connections with the region between the Marne and the upper Loire. They were probably not homogeneous, but they had reached a developed stage of La Tène culture, which was thus introduced into this country by them. Although doubtless some slight infiltration of this culture into the south-eastern districts was also going on, it was these Iron Age B people who were mainly responsible for the introduction into this country of what is popularly recognized as Celtic art. Their bronzes and pottery were frequently decorated with scroll work and those stylized "palmette" patterns which survived even the long Roman occupation, and revived again in the dark ages before the Norman Conquest.

The Iron Age B people also constructed hill forts, with more elaborate fortifications, and they preferred, where stone was available, to build unmortared stone ramparts rather than mere earthworks. Among the largest of their forts are Hembury in Devon and Ham Hill in Somerset. But the most stupendous of their fortifications is *Maiden Castle* (Plate 4), where the existing gigantic earthworks were erected about 50 B.C., apparently by refugee chiefs of the Veneti, the Celtic tribe in Brittany, who fled to Britain after the destruction of their fleet by Julius Cæsar in 56 B.C. The Veneti were famous in Gaul for using the sling in warfare, and the sudden multiplication of lines of rampart and ditch seen at *Maiden Castle*, and other large hill forts in Wessex, seems to have been against the attacks by means of this weapon with a range of up to a hundred yards. When used defensively the slingers were stationed on platforms near the gates, and their ammunition was stored in pits behind the defences—one such sling-stone dump at *Maiden Castle* contained over 22,000 selected beach pebbles. Another hill fort in this district in the guardianship of the Ministry of Works is *Blackbury Castle*, near Southleigh in Devon; the triangular outworks to the entrance are probably an addition in later Iron Age times to the single bank and ditch of the original camp.

Perhaps the most interesting relics of these people in southern England are the lake villages of Glastonbury and Meare, where the most highly developed products of their art have been discovered. These are now mostly preserved in the Taunton and Glastonbury Museums. Open villages of this period are also fairly numerous in Cornwall, generally within the shelter of a hill fort. One such village is in our guardianship, namely, *Chysauster,* about three miles north of Penzance. This seems to have originated in the first century B.C., and it continued in occupation under the Roman Empire up to the third century A.D. The houses consist of oval enclosures of thick, dry-built masonry, forming an open court from which various rooms open: the shape is common to other Cornish villages of this type. *Chysauster*, like other such villages, contains a curious underground chamber known locally as a "Fougou". Parallels to these are found in Scotland and Ireland.

It is to the period of Iron Age B that the great age of the tin mines of Cornwall belongs. Herodotus had heard of the "Tin Islands" in the fifth century, and merchants from the Greek City of Massilia (Marseilles) were certainly engaged in this trade in the fourth and third centuries, and the archæological evidence seems to prove that the great period for the exploitation of Cornish tin was during the last two or three centuries B.C. It is important to remember that the Romans did not mine the tin of Cornwall before A.D. 250 and then only very little, and that their occupation of the Duchy was late and only very partial. Neither Strabo nor Pliny mentions tin as an export of Cornwall in the first century A.D., and Cæsar only heard of it at second-hand from the Kentish tribes, who told him it came from the "interior".

C. The third great invasion of the Iron Age took place about 75 B.C. The invaders were of the mixed Celto-Germanic people known as the Belgæ, whom we have already noticed in the region of the lower Rhine. They had spread over north-eastern France during the preceding centuries, and had absorbed the culture of La Tène, and early in the first century B.C. some of them crossed to Britain, where they conquered the south-eastern districts (with the exception of Sussex), subduing the earlier Iron Age A peoples.

Between 58 and 56 B.C. when Julius Cæsar was engaged in conquering Gaul, the Belgæ of Britain on several occasions sent help to their kindsmen across the Channel against Rome. This led to Cæsar's two invasions of 55 and 54 B.C., the first being merely a reconnaissance, and the second a punitive expedition. In his second invasion Cæsar penetrated beyond the Thames, where he defeated Cassivellaunus, chief of the Belgic tribe of the Catuvellauni, to whose command the other Belgic British chieftains had submitted in order to oppose the invader. After his victory Cæsar imposed tribute on the British tribes, but it does not appear that any serious attempt was made to collect it: his invasions, however, seem to have achieved their object, and we hear no more of British interference in Gaul. On the contrary, the Roman conquest of Gaul led to a fresh invasion of Britain by Belgic refugees from the Roman power. One Commius, chief of the Atrebates (who give their name to Arras) had been a loyal ally of Cæsar in Gaul; but in 52 B.C. he joined the great Gallic rebellion against Rome, and on its failure he became an outlaw, and early in 50 B.C. he escaped to Britain with numerous followers from his own Atrebates and other Belgæ. He established himself in the country between South-ampton Water and the Thames, and apparently brought it under the rule of himself and his sons.

Of monuments under our guardianship the only one which can with some confidence be ascribed to the time of the Belgæ is the *White Horse* at Uffington. This, the earliest of the white horses cut in the turf of the chalk downs, bears a striking resemblance to the horse that appears on the reverse of so many pre-Roman British coins. These coins are decadent imitations of the gold staters of Philip of Macedon, stamped with a head in profile on the obverse and a horsed chariot on the reverse. These staters became current at Rome as the result of the Roman conquest of Macedonia 194-167 B.C., and were introduced into Gaul by Roman trade in the second half of that century. There they were imitated by the Gallic tribes, and from Gaul these imitations in decadent form spread to Britain, but were not struck there till the arrival of the Belgæ. These coins were not, however, the earliest to be struck in this country; for early in the first century B.C. a barbarous tin coinage was in use by the Iron Age A peoples in south-east Britain; it survived the Belgic invasions. The Uffington *White Horse* is typical of one stage of the devolution of the coin design based originally on the horsed chariot of the Macedonian stater, and is thus almost certainly to be attributed to the people who first struck these coins in this country. (*Bratton Camp* also has an adjacent White Horse. In its present form it dates from the eighteenth century, but it is possible that there was originally another Belgic horse on or near this site.)

So far from the Belgæ being primitive savages (as has erroneously been deduced from the pages of Cæsar) there can be no doubt that they possessed a high degree of very real civilization when they reached these coasts. During the century 50 B.C.-A.D. 50, the progress in the southern parts of Britain was very rapid. Though the Belgic invaders built hill forts these seem mostly to be purely military works concentrated on frontiers rather than the tribal capitals of the earlier stages of the Iron Age. Their urban centres were on plateau sites such as Silchester, which was perhaps Commius' capital, in north Hampshire, or the successive capitals of the Catuvellaunian princes at *Verulamium* (St. Alban's) and Colchester. With this also goes the tendency towards larger social groups than the tribe. Already in Cæsar's time Cassivellaunus was recognized as leader in war of all the tribes affected by the invasion: after Cæsar's departure he consolidated this position, and early in the first century A.D. his grandson Cunobelin ruled over the chieftains of the whole of south-eastern England (with the exception of Sussex), even including most of the dominions which had belonged to Commius and his sons. British princes abandoned their old barbarous coinage, and took to striking coins on the Roman model with Roman inscriptions, and called themselves by the Latin title *Rex*, and goods of Roman manufacture were quite common in the markets of Belgic Britain.

Cunobelin's long reign (about A.D. 5-40) was a period of more or less peaceful development, though it is clear that the expansion of his rule made him enemies among other Belgic chieftains, and that the growth of Belgic power was a menace to the non-Belgic peoples of Sussex and the west, and caused them to look for succour towards Rome.

I have written in the above survey of successive waves of invasion which imposed new cultures and ways of life on South and Eastern Britain, cultures which were only slowly absorbed in the North and West. In view of the probability that few of these invasions other than the first Belgic were undertaken by large numbers in the nature of any mass migration, and also of the probability that few women accompanied their menfolk in the hazard of the seas, it is almost certain that by the close of the prehistoric period the population of Britain was already of very mixed race. Doubtless when the Romans came the form of speech had become Celtic universally, but that the inhabitants were mainly or even predominantly Celtic in race is unlikely. Cæsar himself noted the contrast between the tall fair-haired elements and the short dark-haired. Clearly many strains from neolithic and Early Bronze Age times survived in the ranks below the aristocracy of Celtic warrior chiefs.

Throughout prehistoric times the greater part of the lowlands and valleys of England were densely forested, and until iron came into general use man could make little headway against the forest. Until the Iron Age invasions of the last three centuries before Cæsar the potter's wheel and wheeled vehicles were unknown, horses and cattle were both small in stature compared with our present domestic animals. But the earliest neolithic occupants of the *Avebury* area already possessed domestic cattle, horses, pigs, goats and hunting dogs. All through prehistoric times the bow and arrow was the principal weapon used in hunting, and the use of flint arrowheads lasted for many centuries after the first introduction of bronze.

Immense strides have been made in the art and science of archæology in recent years in Britain as elsewhere. But, though the available data are increasing rapidly, it is still too soon for us to be able to formulate those general deductions which are ultimately required to write our island story with either completeness or confidence. It is only by being able to collect fully authenticated material from many different areas of Western Europe that we can hope to paint that complete picture of which

Plate 5. RICHBOROUGH CASTLE.

Plate 6. PORTCHESTER CASTLE

Plate 7.   Pevensey Castle

Plate 8. OLD SARUM

we can at present only draw the outline sketch. The southern counties of England are particularly rich in prehistoric remains and as much scientific work has been done on them as in any area.

Even *Avebury* and *Stonehenge* present numerous problems the solutions of which are still only tentative. Above all, there is a danger in attempting to isolate any one area of investigation. We must seek to interpret the data revealed by the spade in an area like Southern England in the light of knowledge obtained from places as far apart as Portugal and Denmark, or the Outer Hebrides and the Rhine. Nothing is more remarkable than the wide diffusion of the evidences of similar cultures in our prehistoric periods, and it is only by the scientific collation of these that we can tell at all accurately the story of the earliest colonization of Britain by our remote ancestors.

ROMAN PERIOD

The two invasions of Julius Cæsar belong in effect to the preceding period of British history, and have been described in that context. For nearly a hundred years after them Britain was left alone by the Roman Government, until the peaceful penetration of Roman traders and the hostile rivalries of British chieftains made the time ripe for the annexation which Julius had dreamed of and which Augustus had on two occasions contemplated.

In A.D. 43 the Emperor Claudius gave orders for the invasion and conquest of Britain, and an army of four legions, with auxiliaries, was landed on the coast of Kent under the command of Aulus Plautius Silvanus.

One of their ports of disembarkation was certainly *Richborough* (Portus Rutupiæ) (Plate 5), which is in our guardianship. Here among the successive traces of occupation lasting four centuries can be seen part of the fortifications thrown up by the legions of Aulus Plautius to protect their base on landing. *Richborough* was at that time an island in the estuary of the Stour, and was probably connected with the mainland by a causeway.

The opposition of the non-Belgic to the Belgic tribes was exemplified by Cogidubnus, King of Sussex, who hastened to join the Romans, and as a reward was left in enjoyment of his kingdom till his death. A large inscription is still preserved at Chichester in which he is given the unique title of "King and Legate of the Emperor in Britain".

The main resistance of the Belgic kingdom of the Catuvellauni, though fierce, was soon crushed by the capture of their capital near Colchester (Camulodunum). The subsequent obstinate resistance of Caratacus, Cunobelin's son, in the mountains of Wales does not concern us here. Once the main Belgic power had been broken, the conquest of the south and west followed fairly easily. It was entrusted to the Second Legion, then under the command of the future Emperor Vespasian, who, we are told by Suetonius, captured twenty British hill forts in the course of this campaign. These were no doubt mostly those of the western Belgæ, and must have included Hod Hill in Dorset, where there is a Roman fortified camp in a corner of the Belgic earthwork, and *Maiden Castle*, which the Romans stormed and "slighted".

The Roman conquest though rapid was complete. Within five years of the first invasion the Romans were mining the lead of the Mendips, and there was no further military activity south of the Thames for nearly 250 years.

The achievements of the Roman Empire during that period were the victories of peace. Local government was instituted, according to the Roman practice in Gaul, on the basis of the existing tribal divisions, each tribe having its own territory with a capital town. In southern England there were six such tribal states—the Cantii of Kent, capital Canterbury (Durovernum), the Atrebates of Berkshire, Surrey, and north Hampshire, capital Silchester (Calleva, probably Commius' old capital), the Belgæ of Hampshire and Somerset, capital Winchester (Venta), the Regni of Sussex, capital Chichester (Noviomagus), the Durotriges of Dorset, capital Dorchester (Durnovaria), and the Dumnonii of Devon, capital Exeter (Isca). Five of these six towns are covered by modern cities, but the sixth, Silchester, is almost bare of modern buildings and was systematically excavated in the last years of the nineteenth century. Though it is now buried once more, an excellent idea of it can be gained from Reading Mudeum, where most of the finds are preserved and where there are plans and models of the buildings, including one of a Christian church, probably of the fourth century, the only one hitherto known in Roman Britain. The walls of Silchester still stand above ground. They have not yet been accurately dated, but by analogy should belong to the late first or early second century.

Another Roman town of importance in the south is Bath (Aquæ Sulis), which was apparently only a health-resort, and not the capital of any tribe; but it contains, in its baths, one of the most interesting monuments of the Roman era in the country. They are in the custody of the Corporation of Bath.

Another feature of the flourishing period of the Roman Empire in Britain is the Villas, which are numerous in the southern counties. Among the largest may be mentioned Folkestone in Kent, Bignor in Sussex, and Brading in the Isle of Wight. It is, of course, a mistake to suppose that these villas were inhabited by immigrant Romans from Italy. They were the farms and houses of well-to-do British-born gentry, whose ancestors had fought against Cæsar and Claudius; and it was the greatest achievement of the Empire to turn such people into Romans.

Perhaps the most important factor in the "Romanizing" of the country was the road-system. The great majority of the main Roman roads were laid out by military engineers to meet the needs of the army during the period of conquest. This is exemplified in eastern Kent where four roads from the four ports of *Reculver*, *Richborough*, Dover, and Lympne converge on Canterbury, whence the road now known as Watling Street (most of which is still in use) proceeds direct to the crossing of the Thames at Southwark. But when once their military purpose had been served the roads remained as a civilizing agency of the first importance, and it is worth notice that the centre of the road-system was London. In south England, apart from those highways already mentioned, roads ran from London to Chichester and on to *Portchester*, and from London to Silchester, where four routes diverged to Gloucester, Bath, Dorchester and Exeter, and Winchester and the coast. Few Roman roads are more striking to-day than the section of the Dorchester road south-west of Salisbury striding over Oakley Down near Pentridge in north Dorset, and cutting through Bronze Age barrows in its path. This section is scheduled as an Ancient Monument. The road-system terminated for the first two centuries of this period at Exeter, which represented for so long the limit of Roman penetration in that direction. Cornwall remained outside the area of Roman administration till the third century.

Meanwhile, during this peaceful period the original base-camp at *Richborough* had undergone several changes. Shortly after the first landing the site became a military depôt and numbers of large store-houses and other buildings in timber were erected. Towards the end of the first century these buildings were swept away and a great monument was built, probably to commemorate the conquest of Britain. The huge concrete foundation 30 feet deep of this monument remains, and is a prominent feature of the site. The monument was cased with slabs of imported Italian marble, and bore an inscription, too little of which has up to the present been found to make a restoration possible. During the second and third centuries civilian buildings of the kind common in other towns grew up in the shadow of it.

In the latter part of the third century military activity again became necessary in the south owing to the raids of Saxon pirates, and as a result a small fort was established at *Richborough* around the monument; the triple ditches of this fort have been excavated and are now left open. Shortly afterwards, in the later years of the same century, a larger area was enclosed by the existing stone fort, the walls of which remain up to 25 feet high in places, and are no less than 11 feet thick. Its plan was rectangular, and the wall was strengthened by turrets, and surrounded by a double ditch. A comprehensive selection of the important finds made during the recent excavations is shown to the public in the museum erected on the site.

This stone fort at *Richborough* was one of a series of similar forts erected at about this time to guard the east and south coasts from Saxon raids, and which extended from the Wash to Spithead. In the fourth century these were under the command of a special officer with the title of "Count of the Saxon Shore". Three other forts of this Saxon Shore series in the Southern Counties besides *Richborough* are under our guardianship, namely *Reculver* (Regulbium), *Pevensey* (Anderida), and *Portchester* (Portus Adurni).

Reculver, like *Richborough*, seems to have been built in the later years of the third century, despite the earlier look of its walls; there was, however, previous occupation of the site from the late Iron Age onwards. *Pevensey* (Plate 7), too, seems contemporary with *Richborough* and *Reculver* but is oval, not rectangular, and its walls are provided with solid semi-circular bastions. The material is mainly flint rubble and green sandstone, with bonding courses of brick and ironstone. As late as 1147 when *Pevensey* was besieged by King Stephen, it proved impregnable because of the strength of "its most ancient walls". William the Conqueror had landed at *Pevensey*, and before the end of the eleventh century the Norman Lord de Aquila had begun the construction within the large Roman fortress of an inner bailey and keep, but clearly it was the old Roman curtain then still intact which made the place impregnable in those days.

The existing appearance of *Portchester* (Plate 6) is even more impressive than *Pevensey*. In fact, next to Hadrian's Wall it is the most remarkable Roman monument in Britain. High tides in Portsmouth Harbour still reach the foot of the great Roman walls with their hollow semicircular bastions. *Portchester*, like *Richborough,* is rectangular, and is one of the largest of the Saxon Shore forts, containing within its walls an area of about eight acres. The north-west corner is now filled by the twelfth century Norman keep and extensive remains of the mediæval castle, and the south-west by the beautiful twelfth-century church of an Augustinian Priory—now the Parish Church. But large though these later works are, the great expanse of the Roman fortress surrounded in the main by its original walls and towers constitutes one of our finest monuments.

There are the remains of another Saxon Shore fort at Lympne and there was one at Dover, but its site is now covered by the modern town. There is, however, another Roman building there which is in our guardianship, and that is the *lighthouse* which serves as the tower of the Saxon church of St. Mary in Castro. Till the eighteenth century another similar tower stood on the western side of the harbour, but it fell into ruin. (It appears that the western lighthouse was contemporary with the Saxon Shore system, but the existing one may well be much earlier.) Underlying the mediæval castle of *Carisbrooke* in the Isle of Wight are the walls of a rectangular Roman fort probably of late date.

Two other monuments of the Roman period are in the guardianship of the Ministry of Works. These are the small temple on *Jordan Hill*, Weymouth, and the similar temple within the great Iron Age fort of *Maiden Castle*. The latter was of a type known as Romano-Celtic which is commonly found both in Gaul and in Britain. It had a priest's house adjacent and is of interest as it was completed not earlier than 367, and was repaired later than 379. The *Jordan Hill* temple was unscientifi-

cally excavated in 1843, and it is not now possible to assign a
definite date to it, but the presumption from the coins and
pottery found is that it also was occupied in the later years of
the fourth century. This recrudescence of paganism in the last
years of official Roman rule, and in the case of *Maiden Castle*,
the re-use of a pre-historic earthwork for the purpose, is a most
interesting phenomenon, which has a parallel at Lydney in
Gloucestershire.

In 410 the usurper Constantine III withdrew the troops from
Britain to fight for the throne of the Empire, and it is unlikely
that they ever returned. The self-governing communities of
Britain were told by the legitimate Emperor Honorius to make
shift for themselves, and to defend their land as best they could
against Pictish and Saxon invaders. That they held out for
over a century with no help from outside, and went down
fighting speaks well for the vitality of Roman culture in Britain.
Italy itself succumbed to Theodoric the Ostrogoth before
Roman Britain was overrun by the Saxons.

It is to this age that Arthur and his knights belong, and we
are getting out of the realm of history into that of romance.
Our knowledge of fifth and even sixth century England
derivable both from written record and from the spade of the
archæologist is still sparse and meagre, and we do not get back
to any real certainty until the arrival of the Christian missionaries
both from Papal Rome and from Ireland and Wales at the end
of the sixth century. And that is the beginning of our mediæval
rather than the continuance of our Roman past.

MEDIÆVAL PERIOD

It has been possible so far to relate the monuments to brief
historical surveys, but now that the mediæval period has been
reached it will be more convenient to readers to depart from
this plan, partly because it is clearly impossible to compress
even a summary of the history of our southern counties from
the Saxon invasions to the Renaissance into the compass of this
guide, and partly because the monuments of this long period,
with its manifold developments of religious and secular architecture, do not lend themselves to that treatment, since they
frequently exhibit the differing styles of four or five centuries.

The mediæval monuments will therefore be dealt with in two main divisions—the Anglo-Saxon period, and the period from the Norman Conquest to the Renaissance, and instead of a history illustrated by the archæological remains, only so much historical introduction will be given as is necessary to an understanding of the individual monuments referred to in this survey.

ANGLO-SAXON PERIOD

The Saxon invasion and settlement of our southern counties emerged in history in the Kingdom of Kent, and somewhat later in the leadership of the Kingdom of Wessex. Cornwall and the greater part of Devon continued its Romano-Celtic civilization independently until the harrying of the country by King Egbert in the ninth century. Never effectively Romanized, Cornwall has a history of its own, with contacts with Ireland on the one hand and Brittany on the other (as during the prehistoric period), rather than with Saxon England throughout the greater part of the Dark Ages. That King Mark, Tristram and Iseult are historical Cornish personages to be seen dimly through the distorting spectacles of later mediæval legend is probable, and Arthur may well have been a real hero of the last days of the Romano-British struggles against the Saxons. His peculiar connection with Cornwall is probably due to his memory being preserved in the one part of southern Britain which was not overrun by the invaders.

On the exposed promontory of *Tintagel* in Cornwall stand the ruins of a twelfth and thirteenth-century Norman castle, but recent excavation has proved that long before these constructions the site was occupied by an important Celtic monastic settlement, which was founded about A.D. 500 and lasted until the middle of the ninth century. This romantic site is now in the guardianship of the Ministry of Works, and though it has no authentic connection with Arthur, the remains of the early Celtic monastery, so far unique in the south of England, are of the greatest interest and importance.

Two works remaining from the period of the Saxon conquest may be mentioned here, though they are not in our guardianship. These are the two earthworks known as Bokerley Dyke and Wansdyke. The best stretch of Bokerley Dyke is to be seen where it crosses the Salisbury-Blandford road near Woodyates. This gigantic defensive earthwork runs for about nine miles from a point in Cranborne Chase to the top of Blagdon Hill in Hampshire, and for nearly two miles forms the boundary between that county and Dorset. The ditch is on the north and east side of the bank. Wansdyke runs from the Bristol Channel near Portishead in an easterly direction and terminates in the neighbourhood of Hungerford in Berkshire: its ditch is on the north side. These two earthworks were thus designed to defend the country to the south and west. Bokerley Dyke has been proved to have been first made in the late fourth century, during the Roman period, perhaps during the great Pictish invasion of A.D. 367, but it was restored and enlarged considerably later, and in this form dates from the earlier period of the Teutonic invasions of the fifth century. Wansdyke, which is of much the same date, can be well seen near Beckhampton, in Wiltshire.

At the other end of our region—in eastern Kent—the Ministry of Works is guardian of three monuments of this period witnessing the earliest developments of Christianity among the Saxons. In the latter half of the sixth century the culture of Kent was a thing apart from that of the rest of England. The magnificent collection of Kentish jewellery and other objects from Faversham now in the British Museum attests the superiority in design and craftsmanship of such articles in the possession of the dwellers in east Kent over those in other parts of England at that time. Now we have it on Bede's authority that Kent and the Isle of Wight were colonized by Jutes rather than by Saxons, from whom they differed considerably. But it has been suggested with considerable probability that the Jutish overlords of east Kent, with their principal capital at Canterbury, came to our shores not directly from Jutland but after a considerable temporary settlement on the middle Rhine, where they were in touch (and in England they remained in touch) with the Danube and oriental trade. Suffice it to say that associated finds at Faversham included large cowrie shells of a type only known in the Indian Ocean.

In 593 Ethelbert, King of Kent, married the daughter of Caribert, King of the Franks, and was recognized as overlord of all the Anglo-Saxon kingdoms south of the Humber. Soon after this marriage with a Christian princess from the Continent he erected for her the still existing Church of St. Martin on the eastern outskirts of Canterbury, where in 597 he was himself baptized by St. Augustine.

Apart from this Church of St. Martin, there are in close vicinity on the ground which was later covered by the Norman *Abbey Church of St. Augustine,* the remains of three churches dedicated to SS. Peter and Paul, to Our Lady and to St. Pancras, all dating from the early seventh century. In the first of these three excavation has revealed the empty tombs of six of the first Archbishops of Canterbury, and of several of the Kentish kings.

On this site developed the Benedictine *Abbey of SS. Peter, Paul and Augustine,* and shortly before the Norman Conquest the Saxon Abbot Wulfric pulled down parts of the first two churches, and began to build a great rotunda to join them into a single church. This work was unfinished at the time of the Conquest, and the first Norman Abbot abandoned the scheme and built a Norman church of usual plan over the Saxon foundations. These foundations have been excavated and can now be seen, and the site has been handed over to the Ministry of Works by St. Augustine's Missionary College, which occupies part of the site of the Abbey.

Visible from a great distance there still stand the gaunt twin towers of *Reculver Church,* built inside the Roman Saxon Shore fort at the mouth of the Wantsum, through which ships could sail as late as Tudor times between Thanet and the mainland of Kent. These two towers are the sad remnants of a large Norman church built in the twelfth century and enlarged in the thirteenth, the greater part of which was wantonly destroyed by the deliberate action of the then vicar and his churchwardens in 1809. The towers were saved by purchase by Trinity House on account of their value as beacons for mariners. Beneath and incorporated in the Norman church are the remains of a most important Saxon church founded by King Egbert of Kent in A.D. 669. It consisted of an aisleless nave, about 37 feet long, and a chancel ending an apse polygonal without and round within. The nave was separated from the chancel by an arcade resting on two lofty stone columns now happily preserved in the eastern crypt of Canterbury Cathedral. On either side of the nave there was a rectangular chamber. The walls were built of flint with bands of Roman brick, and the floor was of a pink mortar. It was enlarged in Saxon times. The whole site is now under the guardianship of the Ministry of Works, and the foundations of the Saxon Church are exposed. A notable feature of the church was a great stone cross which stood in front of the arcade dividing the nave from the chancel:

it is stated by Leland to have been 9 feet high. It consisted of a cross on a round column, carved with bold figures of Christ and the Apostles. Some fragments of this fine sculpture may be seen preserved in the neighbouring modern church of Hillborough. Everything would seem to point to a seventh century date for this exceptional work—the only early sculpture in the south of England that can rank in excellence with the great Anglian crosses of Bewcastle in Cumberland and Ruthwell in Dumfriesshire of near the same date. The reckless destruction of so much of Reculver Church as recently as 140 years ago is one of our greatest archæological losses in the south of England.

Very fragmentary remains of another Saxon church of pre-Conquest date stand within the walls of the Roman Saxon Shore fort of *Richborough*. *Richborough* is the traditional site of the landing of St. Augustine in 597, and the chapel was probably erected to commemorate that important event, at a time when the tradition had become well-established. A stone reputed to bear the impression of St. Augustine's foot, made when he stepped on shore, was kept in the Chapel, which in consequence was much frequented by pilgrims. It was rebuilt in the twelfth century, and continued in use until the sixteenth.

Well preserved remains of an important Saxon church have recently been uncovered at *Muchelney,* Somerset, east of the piers of the crossing of the Norman Abbey. It has a chancel ending in a semicircular apse with a polygonal external face. A bench 1 foot wide round the inner face of the apse is a most unusual feature. Three steps separated the chancel from the nave, which appears to have been destroyed when the foundations for the Norman pier arcades were laid. On the upper step is a re-used plain grave slab. The walls are carefully built of lias stone, and the character of the apse dates it to the eighth century and, like the Saxon church of Glastonbury, its foundation may be ascribed to King Ina, 688-726.

There are no monuments of the Viking or Danish period in our guardianship in the southern counties which were the scene of Alfred's resistance to the invaders, but in Cornwall there is in our custody an interesting monument of the ninth century, namely, *"King Doniert's" inscribed stone,* near St. Cleer. This is part of a granite cross-shaft 4 feet 6 inches high, ornamented with carved panels of interlaced pattern of the type common at this period, and bearing the inscription DONIERT ROGAVIT PRO ANIMA. Doniert is believed to be the same as Durngarth, King of Cornwall, who is reputed to have been drowned in the River Fowey about A.D. 870. With it is part of another cross-shaft with similar decoration.

To the last century before the Norman Conquest belongs the *Church of St. Mary in Castro* at Dover, which is maintained by the Ministry of Works since it is used as the garrison church. It dates originally from about A.D. 1000. In the eighteenth century it became desecrated, and was used as a barrack store, but in 1860 it was over-restored and tastelessly redecorated by Sir Gilbert Scott, and was re-consecrated in 1862.

THE MIDDLE AGES

Our mediæval monuments, from the Norman Conquest to the Renaissance, can be most conveniently treated by subdivision into ecclesiastical and secular building.

1. ECCLESIASTICAL BUILDINGS

When compared with the numerous and fine monastic buildings in our guardianship in other regions, the southern counties are poor. In this district monastic churches were either, like Romsey, Christchurch, Sherborne, and Malmesbury, converted into parish churches, or were ruthlessly destroyed.

There are only five religious houses in the southern counties the remains of which are in our guardianship, though we have a few other small buildings which were connected with monastic foundations and which will be included under this head. The beautiful little Norman Priory Church of Portchester, though within the walls of the Roman fort, is not in our care, since it is the parish church.

It has been seen from *Tintagel* that monastic communities existed in the old Celtic Church, which in the Dark Ages of the Teutonic invasions kept alive in the west the Christianity of the Roman Empire, and in the north of England similar institutions were produced by the Anglian people of Northumbria under the influence of the Celtic missionaries from Iona. But in the south of England the regular rule of St. Benedict was introduced almost immediately by the missionaries from Rome, and numerous Benedictine foundations existed before the Norman Conquest.

The Saxon *Abbey of St. Augustine at Canterbury* has already been mentioned. Here as elsewhere the Normans super-imposed over the Saxon foundations a far more grandiose structure. Remains of the crypt and painted decoration on the plaster walls of its chapels are still visible, and the plan of the cloister and monastic buildings has been exposed by excavation.

Another Benedictine House in our guardianship which dates originally from Saxon times is *Muchelney Abbey* in Somerset, near Langport (Plate 17). It stands on what is really an island in Sedgemoor, and in time of flood is still liable to be cut off from all communication by land. According to one tradition it was founded and endowed by King Athelstan in expiation of the murder of the Atheling Edwin in 933, but definite evidence has now been found that it was a good deal older and its foundation, as stated above, is with more probability ascribed to King Ina, 688-726. It was never a house of any great wealth or importance, and at the dissolution there was an abbot, a prior, and only eight monks.

The remains of the Saxon church here have already been described. Of the later church only the lower courses of the north and east walls have survived, and these belong to the Norman building of about 1100, though in the fifteenth century the eastern apse was destroyed and a new and longer presbytery erected. The rest of the church, the cloister, and the east and west ranges have mostly been robbed down to the footings, but their outlines have been recovered and are marked out in the turf. The main portions now standing consist of the Rere-dorter, originally of the twelfth century, but altered in the thirteenth, which stands by itself, and a block comprising the south walk of the cloister, part of the Frater, the Kitchen, and the Abbot's Lodging. These buildings in their present form date from the late fifteenth and early sixteenth centuries, and contain some magnificent work of that period. After the dissolution the Abbey and its lands were granted to Edward Seymour, Earl of Hertford, and later Duke of Somerset. The Abbot's Lodging was used as a dwelling-house, and the other buildings fell steadily into decay.

Three other religious houses in our guardianship are all of later date, and belong to Orders which were not instituted till the twelfth century. They are not among the earliest foundations of those Orders.

Cleeve Abbey in Somerset was a daughter house of Revesby Abbey in Lincolnshire, and was founded towards the close of the twelfth century for monks of the Cistercian Order by William de Roumara, third Earl of Lincoln. Its church, of which only the foundations remain, was of typical Cistercian plan, with a short, square-ended presbytery. The claustral buildings, however, are amongst the most complete to be seen in England, the east and south ranges retaining their roofs and floors. The refectory, with a fine timber roof, was rebuilt in the later Middle Ages on the normal Benedictine plan as a first-floor hall parallel to the south alley of the cloister, and replaced an earlier refectory built at right angles to the cloister in the normal Cistercian manner. The buildings contain some notable floor-tiles and wall-paintings. The gatehouse was rebuilt by the last Abbot, William Dovell, who surrendered the Abbey in 1537.

Netley Abbey (Plate 18) on Southampton Water was also a Cistercian House, a daughter of Beaulieu across the Water, and was founded in 1239 by King Henry III. Though not of the first rank as regards size, it is very complete, and of quite exceptional beauty. The ruins are extensive, and the walls of the church and of the greater part of the conventual buildings are still standing. Although later in date than most Cistercian foundations, the orthodox ground plan of the Order was adhered to in the main, though with some modifications which had already been found desirable in earlier houses. At *Netley*, except for some Tudor alterations made after the dissolution, practically all existing structures date from the middle of the thirteenth century, and few purer or more refined examples of the Early English style at its best remain to us. The delicacy of the tracery of the windows, the plain architectural treatment of the capitals, and the excellence of the masonry make *Netley* one of the most attractive monastic buildings in the country.

Within a few miles of *Netley* are the remains of *Titchfield Abbey* (Plate 16) founded in 1222 by Peter des Roches, Bishop of Winchester, as a house of Premonstratensian Canons. The church was completed and consecrated in 1238. At the dissolution in 1537 it was given by King Henry VIII to Thomas Wriothesley, Earl of Southampton, who immediately began to transform the Abbey into a mansion for himself. The mansion, known as "Palace House", was visited by King Edward VI and by Queen Elizabeth. It was to *Titchfield* that King Charles I fled from Hampton Court in 1647, and there he was taken prisoner by Colonel Hammond, and thence conveyed to *Carisbrooke Castle*.

Of the thirteenth-century church only part of the nave survives, as transformed into his Palace House by Wriothesley, who pulled down the choir and south transept. The cloister, which was on the north side, became the courtyard of the house, and the nave became the south wing. It was cut through the middle to form the great gate of the mansion; turrets were added, and Tudor windows and fireplaces inserted in the nave walls. The nave thus transformed is now almost the only part standing above ground, but many fine monastic tiles of the fourteenth-century paving of the cloister walks may still be seen *in situ*. Much of the detail of the entrance to the Chapter House also survives, and parts of the thirteenth-century central door-way, with its detached shafts and the Purbeck marble sills of the windows which flanked it can still be seen, while the rest is embedded in the Tudor masonry. This complex of thirteenth-century church and Tudor secular transformation is of very considerable architectural interest.

The great Abbey of Glastonbury, one of the holiest spots in the land, where according to the legend St. Joseph of Arimathea first preached the Christian faith in Britain in the first century, is now again in the charge of the Church of England, but two small buildings which were once the property of the Abbey are in the guardianship of the Ministry of Works. One of these is the *Tribunal* or Court House. The front, with a long window extending the full width of the ground floor room and above it, a characteristic bay window below a cornice and plain parapet was rebuilt by Abbot Bere between 1493 and 1524. Over the entrance are panels containing the Royal arms and a Tudor rose. The fine oak roofs have been restored, and there is some con-temporary linen-fold panelling.

The other of these buildings is the *"Fish House"* not very far distant at Meare. It was probably built in the second quarter of the fourteenth century for the Abbey official in charge of the fishponds. It is a small, plain, rectangular structure with a door and windows of its period.

At *Abbotsbury* in south Dorset the Ministry of Works has taken over the care of the small and beautifully-vaulted chapel on the conspicuous hill-top, which, like so many other hill-tops in the country, is dedicated to St. Catherine. It is of fifteenth century date and was probably served by the adjacent Abbey which, save for its great tithe-barn nearby, has almost entirely disappeared. The eastern gable-end of one of the monastic buildings, however, still stands, and is in the guardianship of the Ministry of Works, and the footings of the north wall of the Abbey Church may be seen in the churchyard of the adjacent Parish church. The two churches were side by side, as was also the case at *Muchelney*.

Another building with monastic connections and now in the charge of the Ministry is the great *barn* at Barton Farm on the outskirts of *Bradford-on-Avon*. It was built in the fourteenth century for Shaftesbury Abbey and is 174 feet long, with four porches and a timber roof of 14 bays.

The Ministry also has in its guardianship two buildings in the southern counties that were formerly establishments of the Order of Knights Templar. On the Western Heights at *Dover* are the foundations of the circular nave of a small twelfth-century church belonging to the Order. The Templars adopted this plan in imitation of the form of the Church of the Holy Sepulchre in Jerusalem, and six other examples belonging to them are known to have existed in England. The other building associated with the Knights Templar is also in Kent, where the first-floor hall and undercroft of their manor-house at *Temple Manor, Rochester,* have survived incorporated in later buildings.

In addition to these monuments that once belonged to the Monastic and Military Orders, three other ecclesiastical buildings are maintained by the Ministry in this area. The earliest in date is the *Garrison Church* at *Portsmouth* which, although considerably altered and much restored, was originally a thirteenth-century hospital dedicated to St. John the Baptist and St. Nicholas. This hospital was founded by Bishop Peter des Roches of Winchester about the year 1214. The vaulted chancel of three bays, originally the hospital chapel, is of great architectural interest and dates from the thirteenth century. It fortunately escaped destruction when the nineteenth-century nave was badly damaged by enemy action in 1941. King Charles II was married to Catherine of Braganza in this church on May 21st, 1662. *Horne's Place Chapel, Appledore,* is a fourteenth-century chapel with undercroft, once forming part of the buildings of a manor-house. In Cornwall, *Dupath Well Chapel,* is an example of a late mediæval well-house built over a holy well.

2. SECULAR BUILDINGS

(i) *Castles*

The castles in the southern counties which are maintained by the Ministry of Works, or are in our guardianship, number twenty-nine. These fall into three groups according to their initial date, namely, Norman, late Fourteenth-Century, and Tudor, and are dealt with under those heads.

(a) Norman

In *Old Sarum* (Plate 8) we have in our guardianship an important monument which dates from early in the reign of William the Conqueror, and is of exceptional scale and interest. It is a fortified town not merely a castle.

There can be little doubt that the natural hill of *Old Sarum* was the site of prehistoric and perhaps of Roman occupation, though little has been found to prove it. That it was an important Saxon settlement seems certain, as it is recorded that King Alfred ordered its fortification to be repaired and King Edgar held a Witan there. It possessed a Royal mint in the days of Canute and Edward the Confessor.

After harrying the north, William the Conqueror assembled his victorious armies at *Old Sarum* in 1070 and disbanded them there. Before 1078 he transferred the ancient Saxon bishopric of Sherborne to Sarisberie, *i.e.*, to *Old Sarum*. From this time date the vast earthworks which we see to-day, transforming the site into an imposing citadel. The first Norman cathedral was completed by Bishop St. Osmund and consecrated in 1092. It was situated in the north-western corner of the fortification. This church, with its eastern apses, was considerably enlarged and given a square east end by Bishop Roger who died in 1139. To his efforts were due the completion of the great tower of the castle. Further additions to all the buildings were made between 1181 and 1188. As long as the Bishop was in charge of castle, cathedral, and city alike, all was well. But when Henry II assumed control of the castle, and appointed his own military Castellan, friction between the military and ecclesiastical authorities soon developed. In 1217 the Dean and Chapter petitioned Pope Honorius III to inquire into their many grievances. The outcome was the foundation in 1220 of the present cathedral nearly two miles south of the great castle. In 1227 the old cathedral was finally abandoned, and thereafter used as a quarry for buildings in the new city. Many of the Norman-worked stones from *Old Sarum* can still be seen built into the wall of the precincts round the close. The castle fell into gradual disuse and decay, and in 1446-7 is described as no longer

Plate 9. Dover Castle

Plate 10.   DOVER, THE CASTLE UPPER CHAPEL IN THE KEEP

Plate 11. CARISBROOKE CASTLE

Plate 12. RESTORMEL CASTLE.

of any value. With the final abandonment of the castle in the fifteenth century, the last inhabitants left for the new city. But for many generations, until the Reform Act of 1832, though without a house or inhabitant, it continued to send two members to the House of Commons by virtue of its early mediæval Charter of Incorporation as a Borough. It was perhaps the rottenest of the famous rotten boroughs, but its story is redeemed by the fact that it sent to Parliament for no less than thirteen years William Pitt, afterwards the great Earl of Chatham.

The grandest Norman keep in the guardianship of the Ministry of Works in the southern counties is that of *Dover Castle* (Plate 9). It is only exceeded in size by the White Tower of the *Tower of London* and the keep at Colchester, and with the possible exception of the former there is no finer or better preserved example of a square Norman keep with all its elaborations of internal planning. The keep, which is 98 by 96 feet at ground level and 83 feet high to wall head, with an additional 12 feet to the turret tops, was built by King Henry II between the years 1181 and 1187. The walls are of exceptional thickness —some 22 feet at the base—and in the thickness of the walls are a quite unusually large number of mural chambers. The great staircase leading up to the main entrance is very fine, and is protected by a forebuilding. This forebuilding contains, near the entrance doorway into the keep and again on the next storey, two superimposed chapels (Plate 10) very richly ornamented with late Norman mouldings. The hall of the keep contains a small collection of armour. In the keep is a well, 3 feet 3 inches in diameter, popularly known as Harold's Well, and it may indeed be much older than the existing keep. Starting at the well-head a number of lead pipes carried the water to various rooms throughout the building, a very unusual arrangement at this early date. The well is clear to a depth of 242 feet, and below that is filled with many more feet of rubbish thrown down at different times, principally by French prisoners during the Napoleonic wars. In addition to the keep, the inner line of ramparts and towers is mainly of twelfth-century date, while the fine outer line, much repaired and altered at different dates, was constructed during the thirteenth century. The Constable's Tower now forming the entrance for visitors, is a fine example of military architecture of the end of that century. The polygonal "Avranches" tower of the early thirteenth century is also interesting.

It was from *Dover Castle* in 1190 that Richard Cœur de Lion and some of his Crusader knights set out for Palestine. It has been continuously garrisoned since the Norman Conquest, and much of its area is now occupied by modern barracks.

Dover is one of the Cinque Ports, famous in mediæval history as being required to furnish ships for the King for the defence of the realm. The other four original Cinque Ports were Hastings, Sandwich, Hythe, and New Romney. To these Rye and Winchelsea, still two of the most charming mediæval towns in England, were added in the thirteenth century. In more recent centuries the Lord Warden of the Cinque Ports, who has combined with this ancient office the Constableship of *Dover Castle*, has been either a member of the Royal Family, or a distingusihed statesman, admiral, or general. His official residence is *Walmer Castle*, which is referred to later.

Brief reference has already been made to the Norman additions to the Roman Saxon Shore fortresses of *Portchester* and *Pevensey*.

The keep at *Pevensey* is of peculiar interest and unique in type. Instead of the usual square Norman keep, we find an irregularly planned structure with numerous apsidal projections or bastions. This is of early date, having been built in the last years of the eleventh or the earliest of the twelfth century. The lord of the castle was then Richer de Aquila, possibly connected with those Norman adventurers who made themselves masters of Sicily and many places in southern and eastern Italy. The gatehouse, walls and bastions of the inner bailey belong to the middle of the thirteenth century and are in the fully developed style of that period.

At *Portchester* (Plate 6) the great Norman keep of ashlar built at the north-west corner of the Roman fort was erected by King Henry II between 1160 and 1172. It is 40 feet square at the base, where the walls are 8 feet thick. It is an admirable example of a large Norman keep both within and without. *Portchester* has always been a Royal Castle, with a Constable appointed by the Sovereign. The walls of the inner bailey south and east of the keep, and the inner moat, were also the work of the twelfth century, but the domestic buildings built against these walls, and the elaborate extensions of the gatehouse and of the drawbridge over the inner moat are mostly the work of the fourteenth century, principally of King Richard II.

Much smaller in scale than these keeps, but of particular interest because of its very early date, is the keep-like tower once attached to the Church of St. Leonard at *West Malling* in Kent, said to have been built by Bishop Gundulf of Rochester (1077-1108) who was also responsible for the building of the *White Tower* in London.

At *Eynsford* in Kent the Ministry are also guardians of a castle which has associations with William of Eynsford, who was involved in a dispute over presentation with Archbishop Thomas à Becket. The castle is of twelfth-century date, and consists of a ditch and a tall curtain wall of flint, without towers, enclosing a polygonal area in which stand the ruins of a rectangular stone hall. It appears to have been repaired after a fire about the middle of the thirteenth-century, and abandoned and dismantled shortly afterwards.

Of all the castles in the guardianship of the Ministry of Works in the southern counties none is more frequented by visitors than *Carisbrooke* (Plate 11) in the Isle of Wight. Its association with King Charles I, who was lodged in its walls by the victorious Parliamentarian forces during the greater part of the last year of his life, has made it a special object of pilgrimage. But, apart from its historic associations, it is one of the most interesting of all our national monuments from an archæological point of view.

On the east and west sides of the great Norman bailey we can still trace the remains of the Roman fort that occupied the site. It was almost certainly the scene of the battle in which Cerdic, King of Wessex, conquered the islanders in A.D. 530. At the Norman Conquest the Isle of Wight was granted to William FitzOsbern, and doubtless the large Norman earthwork motte was his work or that of his son. From 1107 to 1155 the island was held by one Baldwin de Redvers, who built the existing circular or shell keep on the older motte, and enclosed the bailey with a curtain wall, much of which still stands.

The next important builder was the Countess Isabel, daughter of Baldwin de Redvers IV, and widow of one William de Fortibus. She held the castle from 1263 to 1293, and to her we owe the rebuilding of much of the Great Hall, the adjoining Chapel of St. Peter, the Great Chamber, the "New" (in 1275) Chamber of the Countess, and the Well and Well-house nearby.

At the Countess's death the castle was sold to the Crown. The twin-towered gatehouse, still the entrance to the inner bailey of the castle, was added in 1335-36. Towards the end of the fourteenth century William, Earl of Salisbury, who then held the castle, added to the domestic buildings and provided the hall with its present fireplace.

The much restored buildings in the south-east of the bailey were added by Anthony de Wydvill, Lord of the Island, from 1467-1493.

Finally, between 1597 and 1600, new and very much larger lines of defence were made in the Italian manner enclosing the whole of the old castle and its two baileys. In modern times the Governor's apartments and other domestic buildings have been somewhat drastically restored, and the Chapel of St. Nicholas rebuilt from its foundations. The Governor's apartments now house the museum.

The keep of *Farnham Castle* in Surrey was placed under our guardianship by the Bishop of Guildford shortly after that diocese had been carved out of the ancient diocese of Winchester. The earliest structure was probably an earthen motte thrown up by Bishop Walkelin 1070-98, and the castle remained the residence of the Bishops of Winchester until 1927. Parts of it are still used as the residence of their successor the Bishop of Guildford. The great shell keep was built round the motte by Bishop Henry of Blois 1129-71, who also built the triangular bailey in which is the bishop's residence. The steps leading up to the top of the keep date from the time of Bishop Fox 1500-28.

The castle fell into the hands of the French in 1216, but was recaptured next year by the Earl of Pembroke. During the Civil War it changed hands twice, and under Cromwell's rule it was confiscated, and conveyed to one John Godwyn of Bletchingley; but at the Restoration it was given back to the Bishop of Winchester.

Ludgershall Castle, on the road from Andover to Marlborough, is maintained by the Ministry of Works, as it is on War Office property. The earliest record of it in history is in 1141, when the Empress Maud took refuge within its walls. It was a royal castle, and throughout the thirteenth century the King appointed governors who were generally in charge of Marlborough Castle as well. King Edward II, however, seems to have appointed no governors, and the castle fell into decay. Leland (in 1540) describes it as "clene down", and to-day only fragments of masonry remain, but extensive earthworks still mark its site. Ludgershall was a borough, and sent two members to Parliament till 1832.

In 1337 King Edward III made his eldest son, the Black Prince, Duke of Cornwall and thereafter the lands of the Duchy of Cornwall have always been an apanage of the eldest son of the reigning sovereign. King Edward VIII when Prince of Wales placed three castles of the Duchy under our guardianship.

The smallest of these is *Lydford* in Devon. This was originally a Norman earthwork castle of the usual motte and bailey type, on which a rectangular stone keep of two storeys was erected in the second half of the twelfth century. Some internal improvements were effected by Richard, Earl of Cornwall, about 1260. It early lost its military importance, but in the later Middle Ages the lower floor was used as a prison and the upper floor for the Stannary Court, or court of the tin mines of the neighbourhood. This court earned an unenviable reputation for severity—and Browne, the local seventeenth-century poet, wrote:—

> "I oft have heard of Lydford Law
> How in the morn they hang and draw
> And sit in judgment after".

Another castle of Norman origin handed over to our guardianship by the Duchy of Cornwall is *Restormel* (Plate 12), about 1½ miles from Lostwithiel. The circular motte upon which the castle now stands was almost certainly erected about the year 1100 by Baldwin Fitz Turstin, the Sheriff of Cornwall. The masonry gate may also be of this date, but the circular stone keep (125 feet in diameter) dates from about 1200, and rooms and other buildings within it were probably built by Edmund, son of Richard, Earl of Cornwall, at the end of the thirteenth century. To this date belongs also the rectangular chapel projected outwards on the north-east side of the keep. Edward the Black Prince is known to have visited this castle in 1365. It was garrisoned and fought for in the Civil War, being captured by Sir Richard Grenville in 1644, an episode which closes its history. It forms to-day one of the most attractive of our ancient monuments in its woodland setting.

Reference has already been made to the Celtic monastery at *Tintagel* in Cornwall. The name Tintagel first occurs in that famous "history" of Geoffrey of Monmouth in the twelfth century, which clothed the obscure legends of King Arthur and the Knights of the Round Table with the romance of later mediæval chivalry. The name is not Celtic but Norman-French, and its most romantic and impressive situation may have inspired Geoffrey's gifts as a writer of fiction. The castle was, in fact, first built by Reginald, Earl of Cornwall, an illegitimate son of King Henry I who held *Tintagel* and other lands of the earldom from 1140 to 1175.

The visible remains were mostly built between 1236 and 1272 and are due to the efforts of Richard, Earl of Cornwall, the younger brother of King Henry III. It was this Earl of Cornwall who, in 1257, was chosen by the Electors of Germany as King of the Romans, and, though crowned with the silver crown of Germany at Aachen, never attained the full dignity of Holy Roman Emperor to which his ambitions aspired.

The castle fell into disrepair and disuse as a residence as early as the fourteenth century. The narrow cliff-girt site is in itself a formidable fortress, but its weather-beaten masonry walls, while adding to the picturesqueness of the scene, are of no special architectural quality.

Two other West Country castles of this period, which have recently been placed in the guardianship of the Ministry, remain to be mentioned. Very similar to *Restormel* is the well preserved shell-keep of *Totnes Castle*, in Devon, standing on the summit of a hill above the borough of that name. Together with the stone curtain walls, it was built in the twelfth century on the earthworks of a motte and bailey castle that had been erected by Judhael in the time of William I. In the early fourteenth century its walls were reconstructed, but the plan of the twelfth-century work was followed.

Launceston Castle, in Cornwall, known throughout the Middle Ages as Dunheved, was the principal seat of Robert of Mortain, brother of the Conqueror. The present stone defences, however, which include inner and outer wards with curtain walls, and a cylindrical keep on the summit of a high mound, are mainly of the twelfth and thirteenth centuries. The keep is of particular interest, and has points of similarity with the later structure at *Flint* in North Wales. It consists of a cylindrical tower surrounded by a concentric curtain wall, the ground floor space between the two being originally roofed over. As at *Carisbrooke,* it was approached by a steep stairway up the face of the mound.

(b) *Fourteenth Century*

In the southern counties there are three castles of the late fourteenth century in our guardianship. There is a considerable group of these castles in the country, and they belong to the early stages of the transition from the Norman fortress to the Tudor mansion. They are rather fortified residences than castles proper, and though they largely follow the form of their prototype in still making considerable provision for defence, in their internal arrangements they devote more attention to the amenities of civilized life.

The earliest of these is *Nunney Castle* in Somerset (Plate 13) which was built by John de la Mare, who obtained a licence to crenellate from King Edward III in 1373. It consists of a rectangle with round angle towers, and is surrounded by a moat which has been excavated and again filled with water. It was held for the King in the Civil War, but was captured by the Parliament after a one-day siege and the interior was then dismantled. The north wall collapsed in 1910.

Also in Somerset is *Farleigh Castle*, of similar date. Licence to crenellate was granted in 1383 to Sir Thomas Hungerford, and the castle remained for many generations the property of the Hungerford family. It is of a more ambitious plan than Nunney, having features of a castle of earlier date. A curtain wall with round angle-towers surrounds an inner ward which contains the living quarters, and in the outer ward is the chapel, originally the parish church. The castle itself fell into ruin in the eighteenth century, but the chapel is roofed, and contains some fine tombs of the Hungerfords, a fine fifteenth-century iron grille, a Jacobean pulpit, and a black-letter Bible, formerly chained. There are also considerable fragments of mediæval stained glass, and a collection of armour, mostly of the period of the Civil War. All these have now been placed under the guardianship of the Ministry of Works.

Old Wardour Castle, in southern Wiltshire was built by John, Lord Lovel, who obtained licence to crenellate in 1392, and most of the building dates from that period. In plan it is hexagonal, surrounding a central courtyard of the same shape, and there are square bastions flanking the entrance. Such a plan is unique among English castles. In 1547 it came into the possession of the Arundel family, the present owners, and after 1570 Sir Matthew Arundel made several curious additions and alterations in the Elizabethan Renaissance style, which have been attributed to the design of the famous John Thorpe (Plate 19). In the Civil War it was besieged first by the Parliament and then by the Royalists, and during the second siege the whole western wing was blown up, since when the castle has remained a ruin. It is in a lovely setting in a park of the newer Wardour Castle, which was built about a mile away in 1776 to the design of James Paine.

(c) Tudor

During the fifteenth and sixteenth centuries domestic and military architecture parted company, and developed along separate lines.

The increased use of artillery rendered many of the older castles ineffective and new styles of fortification were gradually evolved, particularly for coastal defence. One of the earliest is The Strong Tower, now known as *Dartmouth Castle* (Plate 14). This does not strictly belong to the Tudor period but may be included here, since it has greater affinity with the later castles for coast defence than with the last group we have been considering.

It was erected in 1481 by the Corporation of Dartmouth and provided with gun-ports from the beginning. It remains substantially as it was built, and was handed over to the then Office of Works by the War Office in 1910.

Further additions to the defences of the coast were made in the reign of King Henry VIII. It is probable that *St. Catherine's Castle,* Fowey, and the original smaller fort at *Pendennis,* now called Little Dennis fort, should be attributed to the middle of the reign. Shortly after the Suppression of the Monasteries Henry VIII embarked upon a comprehensive scheme of coastal defence. "Blockhouses" or "bulwarks" were proposed for every haven and at every possible landing place. Many of these were never built, but within the following few years work was proceeding upon a number of small castles and similar works along the coast from Hull to Milford Haven. Most of these are small, low, but very massive structures, often consisting of a central tower with larger circular bastions pierced with wide embrasures for guns.

Two of the finest, namely, *Pendennis* and *St. Mawe's Castles* (Plate 15) in Cornwall were begun in or about 1540 to defend Falmouth Haven, and are still well preserved, and now maintained by the Ministry of Works. They illustrate the King's intention to have the defences erected in the most up-to-date Continental style. Another example of the type is Camber Castle near Rye, which is in ruins. Other similar blockhouse

fortresses of this date which are in our guardianship are *Deal,
Walmer, Hurst* and *Portland Castles,* some of which have been
much altered since their foundation, and *Yarmouth Castle,* Isle
of Wight, which was built at this time, but is rectangular in plan.
Walmer Castle is the official residence of the Lord Warden of
the Cinque Ports. It contains a small collection of historical
relics and the room in which the famous Duke of Wellington
(who held the office of Lord Warden) died in 1852. The
contents of this room and its decoration were either the Duke's
own or, as in the case of the wall-paper and carpet, reproductions
of those installed by him. As a consequence this Wellington
room is an interesting and very complete example of early
Victorian taste.

The coastal defences erected by Henry VIII extended to the
Scilly Isles, where *King Charles's Castle* on Tresco probably
belongs to his reign. It was a low, oblong fort with a semi-
hexagonal western end in which a gun-port still remains. The
entrance doorway was at the eastern end. *Cromwell's Castle,* also
on Tresco, has no connection with the Protector Oliver, but was
one of the forts built on the Islands by Edward VI after the
fall of the Lord Protector Somerset whose brother, Lord
Seymour of Sudeley, had been accused of using the Islands as
a base for acts of piracy. The castle is a high, cylindrical tower,
the upper story of which is pierced with six gun-ports. Both
this and *King Charles's Castle* were intended to protect New
Grimsby Haven.

Later in the sixteenth century these masonry blockhouses
became out of date, and engineers reverted once more to
defences of earth. Ramparts were constructed of soil or
timber, and frequently revetted with sloping walls of stone or
brick. Angular bastions of various forms were added to ensure
command with cross-fire over the whole of the ramparts. This
system was much elaborated by Vauban and others in later
centuries, but some of the earliest examples of the type now to
be seen in this country are the outer defences of *Carisbrooke,*
which were mostly erected between 1597 and 1602, and the
outer defences of *Pendennis Castle* of about 1598. The fortifications of this period were the result of the war with Spain, of
which the best known event is the defeat of the Spanish Armada
in 1588. The *Carisbrooke* works were erected by an Italian,
Federigo Gianibelli, who was responsible also for the Elizabethan
defences of *Berwick-on-Tweed* and the fortifications of Antwerp;

those of *Pendennis* were partially altered in the reign of Charles I and the castle was thus able to withstand a long siege during the Civil War (1646).

Two other works in the Scilly Isles also belong to the end of the sixteenth century when, despite the defeat of the Armada, the prolongation of the war with Spain made coastal defence a matter of concern to Queen Elizabeth. These are the *Old Blockhouse* on Tresco and *Harry's Walls* on St. Mary's. The former is a rectangular gun-platform which once had a parapet pierced with gun-ports, whilst the latter, work on which was practically finished in 1593, was a square fort with bastions at the angles.

(ii) *Houses*

The principal feature of the mediæval English house, whether large or small, was its hall, which served not only as the living-room and dining-room of the whole household, but sometimes as a common dormitory as well. The hall was a single large room, with or without aisles, its floor either at ground-level or raised above an undercroft, and reached from the outside through a doorway set near the end of one of its side walls. It was heated by a central hearth set on the floor or else by a fireplace in one of the walls. At the opposite end to the entrance was a dais where the lord of the manor or master of the household and his family could sit overlooking their dependants who used the body of the hall. These general arrangements were common to the domestic buildings set within mediæval castles and to the unfortified or semi-fortified manor houses of the countryside, and the earliest example which is in the guardian-ship of the Ministry, the *Norman House* at *Christchurch* in Hampshire, was in fact the great hall of the castle there.

It was probably built about 1160 by Richard de Redvers, 2nd Earl of Devon, or by his son Baldwin, and is a two-storeyed stone building with one large room on each floor. The ground-floor room, lighted by loops, has the remains of a newel staircase in one corner. The hall was on the first-floor and access to it was by means of an external flight of steps which has now gone. It had a fireplace in one wall, the fine cylindrical chimney of which has survived, and three round-headed windows, each of two lights, rabbeted for shutters and enriched with chevron ornament. At the south-east angle there is a later mediæval garderobe.

An early development from the primitive hall plan was the addition of a private chamber or solar at the dais end for the use of the lord and his family. An excellent example of this, placed in the guardianship of the Ministry by the National Trust, can be seen at *Old Soar*, near Plaxtol in Kent, where the solar block of a manor house of the Colepepper family, built in the last years of the thirteenth century, has survived almost intact. The site of the great hall is now occupied by an eighteenth-century house, but a remaining corbel shows that it possessed aisles. The solar block consists of three rooms at first-floor level, each standing over an undercroft and grouped at the dais end of the hall. The largest room was the solar itself, reached by a newel staircase in one of its angles, and containing window-seats, a fireplace and a cupboard. It retains its original timber roof of king-post construction. From the north and east angles two smaller rooms project, the former being a garderobe and the latter a chapel.

Later mediæval buildings of domestic character in the guardianship of the Ministry are *Kirkham House* in *Paignton* and the *Maison Dieu* at *Ospringe*.

RENAISSANCE PERIOD

One of the most important buildings of this period in our charge is the *Queen's House* (Plate 20) at Greenwich, built by Inigo Jones.

The old Greenwich Palace, which had been greatly enlarged by King Henry VIII, lay along the bank of the Thames. To the south lay Greenwich Park, which was enclosed with a brick wall by King James I. Between the old Palace Gardens and the park ran a main public road. Queen Anne of Denmark, who had been granted the Manor of Greenwich by her husband James I, proposed to unite the Palace Gardens and the park by a bridge over the road incorporated in a small Italian Palace. The great Inigo Jones was entrusted with the design in 1616, but on the death of the Queen in 1618 the work was stopped. Building operations were resumed by King Charles I, who gave the house to Queen Henrietta Maria. We know that internal decorations were still being carried out in 1637. The old Greenwich Palace was destroyed in the Civil Wars, but the new

Queen's House was saved. Tradition has it that Cromwell intended to occupy it himself. At the Restoration repairs and some alterations were made by John Webb, Inigo Jones' pupil, and Henrietta Maria, the Queen Mother, returned to live in it till her death in 1669. Thereafter it was granted in turn to Queen Catherine of Braganza and Queen Mary of Modena, but neither lived in it. After the Revolution of 1688 it was occupied by successive Rangers of Greenwich Park, who from 1710 to 1729 were the Governors of the Royal Hospital.

In 1806 the *Queen's House* and its gardens were handed over by Act of Parliament to the Royal Naval Asylum, which in 1821 was merged in the Greenwich Hospital School. Thereafter the house was much altered internally for use as quarters for the officers in charge of the school. The gardens were obliterated and the existing stone colonnades were built on either side of the House to connect it with the new wings of the school.

On the removal of the School to Holbrook in Suffolk in 1933, the *Queen's House* was placed in the charge of the then Office of Works as an ancient monument, and the worst of the later disfigurements of the nineteenth century were removed.

By an Act of Parliament of 1934 the use of it was granted to the National Maritime Museum, and both the *Queen's House* and the Museum were opened to the public by Their Majesties King George VI and Queen Elizabeth on April 27th, 1937.

The Entrance Hall is a perfect cube of 40 feet, and retains its original ceiling (though without the paintings with which it was adorned) and projecting wooden gallery. The circular staircase with its fine ironwork balustrade is also of the period of Inigo Jones, as are the elaborate decorations of the ceilings of the two principal north rooms on the first floor: the painting in the one and the carving in the other are very fine examples of the Italian taste of the time.

The colonnades mark the line of the public roadway which ran through the building. It was diverted and blocked in the eighteenth century, but it is still spanned by the original bridge which connected the two separate wings, and by two other bridges added by Webb in 1661.

Inigo Jones occupies a very important place in the history of English architecture and we are fortunate in possessing in the *Queen's House* so charming and historic an example of his work. In spite of many difficulties and some inevitable restoration, every effort has been made to present the internal as well as external appearance of the house as nearly as possible as designed by him and in the form in which it must have been when occupied by Queen Henrietta Maria in the seventeenth century.

Another former Royal residence, namely, *Kew Palace*, is open during the summer to the public visiting Kew Gardens. This red brick building originally known as "the Dutch House", was built by one Samuel Fortrey, a Dutchman, in the reign of King Charles I. His initials and the date 1631 still appear in the pediment over the main doorway. It is of four storeys, and is an interesting example of the Flemish renaissance style of this date, unusual in this country. The house was acquired on lease by King George II for Queen Caroline about 1730. It was later occupied by Frederick, Prince of Wales, and on his death by the Princess Dowager. In 1781 the house was purchased by King George III as a "nursery" for the very numerous Royal children. Later it was occupied by Queen Charlotte, who died there in 1818. Thereafter it remained closed and empty till 1898, when it was first thrown open to the public. Many alterations to the windows, doors, and the interior of the house generally were carried out by Frederick, Prince of Wales, between 1737 and 1748, probably under the supervision of William Kent, the architect and decorative designer. Some of the furniture now in the building dates back to this time, but other pieces, including the pictures, have been given or lent in recent years. They come for the most part from the Royal Collections and the Victoria and Albert Museum, augmented by one or two private gifts.

Another very important building of the same period is *Ham House*, which was given in 1948 by the Tollemache family to the National Trust, which has leased it at a nominal rent to the Ministry of Works. This splendid example of seventeenth-century domestic architecture began as an H-shaped house, built by Sir Thomas Vavasour, whose initials, with the date 1610, appear on the doorway of the north front. A striking feature of the latter are its loggias in the Italian style, reminiscent of those at Holland House; another is the great staircase, with its pierced balustrade and carved trophies. The house was largely given its present form after the Restoration, when it was the home of the Duke of Lauderdale, one of the members of the notorious Cabal. In particular the south ends of the cross-

wings were enlarged and were united by a range of splendid
state-rooms to form a new south front.

Within, the house is remarkable not only for its superb wood-
work and plasterwork decoration, but for the completeness of
its seventeenth-century furnishings, many of which, like the
pictures in the Long Gallery, still occupy the very rooms for
which they were designed, the whole presenting an unrivalled
impression of the rich character of a great Baroque mansion.
These fittings are in the care of the Victoria and Albert Museum.

There remain three other small monuments of the Renaissance period which are maintained by the Ministry of Works,
and these bring us back to coast defence.

At the Restoration of King Charles II certain coastal defences
were again strengthened. The *Citadel* at *Plymouth* was constructed at this time, and its elaborate gate, bearing the date
1670, is in our charge, and it may be compared to the similar
structure at *Tilbury Fort*, on the Thames, which is dated 1682
and is also in the guardianship of the Ministry. Of the same
character but less elaborate are two gates at Portsmouth. The
defences of the town (as opposed to the harbour), consisting of
earthwork and ditch, were planned by King Henry VIII and
executed under Queen Elizabeth. In 1624 they were so
damaged by a storm that in the years following it was proposed
to remove them. They were repaired, however, by both King
Charles I and Cromwell, but after the Restoration a new plan
was drawn up in 1665, and gradually completed, and it is to
this scheme that our two gates belong. *King James' Gate* was
completed in 1687, and the *Landport Gate* (also called St. George's
or the Old Town Gate), which formed the principal entrance
to the town from the harbour, was finished in 1698. This still
stands on its original site, but King James' Gate was re-erected
in its present position when the old defences of Portsmouth
were demolished between 1874 and 1877.

NOTES

At a number of monuments for which guide books are not yet available the Custodian has notes of the history of the building. A plan is also available for inspection by the public without extra charge.

Real photographic postcard views of monuments are also on sale, at buildings marked with an asterisk, further views are in course of production.

Photographs may be taken by visitors without a permit except at buildings occupied by the military. In these cases the assent of the military must be obtained. The use of stand cameras is subject to the discretion of the Custodian.

Admission Fees. These are indicated under each monument.

Children under fourteen years of age are admitted at half price. At monuments generally, parties of twenty or more visitors are admitted, on application to the Custodian, at half price. For parties of eleven to twenty in number, the minimum fee is 2s. 6d., 5s. or 10s.

Standard Hours of Admission are:—

		Weekdays	Sundays
March-April	...	9 a.m.-6 p.m.	2 p.m.-6 p.m.
May-September	...	9 a.m.-8 p.m.	2 p.m.-8 p.m.
October-February	...	9.30 a.m.-4 p.m.	2 p.m.-4 p.m.
		Closed on Christmas Day.	

Variations from the Standard Hours are noted under the particular monument.

BERKSHIRE

Abingdon County Hall

An outstanding example of a seventeenth-century public building. Built between 1677 and 1683 as a Court for the Justices of Assize and a market hall.

Situation. In Abingdon.

Railway Station. Abingdon.

Admission. Not yet open to the public; work in progress.

Donnington Castle, Newbury

The castle was built towards the end of the fourteenth century, and the barbican of that date remains. There are extensive earthwork defences of the time of the Civil War, when the castle was besieged from 1644 to 1646.

Situation. 1 mile north of Newbury.

Railway Station. Newbury.

Hours of Admission. Standard.

Admission Fee. 6d.

Uffington White Horse and Castle

A large Iron Age camp surrounded by a rampart and single ditch. The horse below the camp is cut in the turf and is probably of the same date. At the foot of the hill is the mound known as Dragon's Hill.

Situation. 2 miles south of Uffington.

Railway Station. Uffington.

Admission. At any time without charge.

Wayland's Smithy, Ashbury

A prehistoric burial place consisting of a long earthen mound containing a cruciform chamber, formed of large blocks of stone, in which the human remains were placed.

Situation. 1 mile east of Ashbury.

Railway Station. Shrivenham.

Admission. At any time without charge.

CORNWALL

*Chysauster Ancient Village, Gulval

A British village dating from about 1 B.C. to the third century A.D., consisting of a series of stone houses, each containing a number of rooms. The site has been partly excavated and the walls of the buildings stand several feet high.

Situation. 2½ miles north-west of Gulval.

Railway Station. Penzance.

Hours of Admission. Standard.

Admission Fee. 6d.

Official Guide Book. In preparation.

Dupath Well Chapel, Callington

An almost complete well-house built over a holy well, c. 1500.

Situation. About 1 mile east of the village.

Railway Station. Callington.

Admission. At any time without charge.

Plate 13. NUNNEY CASTLE

Plate 14. DARTMOUTH CASTLE

Plate 15. ST. MAWE'S CASTLE

Plate 16. TITCHFIELD ABBEY

"The Hurlers" Stone Circles, Minions

Three prehistoric stone circles in a line; one of the best examples of this type of monument in the south-west.

Situation. ½ mile north-west of Minions.

Railway Station. Liskeard.

Admission. At any time without charge.

King Doniert's Inscribed Stone, St. Cleer

Part of a cross-shaft decorated with interlaced pattern and inscribed "DONIERT ROGAVIT PRO ANIMA". Doniert was probably the same as Durngarth, King of Cornwall in the latter half of the ninth century.

There is also part of another cross-shaft with similar decoration.

Situation. 1 mile north-west of St. Cleer.

Railway Station. Liskeard.

Admission. At any time without charge.

Launceston Castle

A fine castle overlooking the town of Launceston. It was the chief seat of Robert of Mortain, brother of William I, but the present stone defences, which include inner and outer wards with curtain walls, and a cylindrical keep on the summit of a high mound, are mainly of the twelfth and thirteenth centuries. The castle was taken by the Parliamentarians in 1646 and later slighted.

Situation. In Launceston.

Railway Station. Launceston.

Hours of Admission. Standard.

Admission Fee. 6d.

Official Guide Book. In preparation.

*Pendennis Castle

A well-preserved castle erected by Henry VIII for coast defence. It was enlarged by Elizabeth. During the Civil War in 1646 it was besieged by the Parliamentary Army under General Fairfax; the siege lasted five months, the garrison capitulating and marching out with colours flying.

Situation. About 1 mile south-east of Falmouth.

Railway Station. Falmouth.

Hours of Admission. Standard.

Admission Fee. 6d.

Official Guide Pamphlet. 3d.

*Restormel Castle.   (Pl. 12)   26·vi·'62   Very fine site

Very interesting remains of a castle begun in the twelfth century, but little of this period now exists, the curtain wall having been built about 1200 replacing the earlier wooden defences. There were probably wooden buildings inside the curtain wall in the first instance, but these were superseded by stone structures towards the end of the thirteenth century.   The surroundings are picturesque.

Situation.   About 1½ miles north of Lostwithiel.
Railway Station.   Lostwithiel.
Hours of Admission.   Standard.
Admission Fee.   3d.
Official Guide Pamphlet.   3d.

Beautifully looked after
Grass & Rhododendrons.

St. Breock Downs, monolith

A fallen granite monolith of prehistoric date, about 16 ft. in length.
Situation.   On St. Breock Downs, 3¾ miles south-south-west of Wade-bridge.
Railway Station.   Wadebridge.
Admission.   At any time without charge.

St. Catherine's Castle, Fowey   26·vi·'62

A fort erected in the reign of Henry VIII for the defence of the harbour.
Situation.   ¾ mile south-west of Fowey.
Railway Station.   Fowey.
Admission.   At any time without charge.

Only a little wall left.

*St. Mawe's Castle.   (Pl. 15)

A fine castle erected by Henry VIII for coast defence.   It consists of a central tower with three semicircular bastions.
Situation.   2 miles east of Falmouth across the estuary.
Railway Station.   Falmouth.
Hours of Admission.   Standard.
Admission Fee.   6d.
Official Guide Pamphlet.   3d.

*Tintagel Castle

The remains of a mediæval castle standing in a picturesque position overlooking the sea.   It was built in the middle of the twelfth century by Reginald, Earl of Cornwall, and has now been divided into two parts by the erosion of the sea.
On the headland there are also the remains of a Celtic monastery of the fifth to the ninth centuries, similar in type to other examples in Ireland and Wales.
Situation.   ½ mile north-west of Trevena.
Railway Station.   Camelford.
Hours of Admission.   Standard.
Admission Fee.   6d.
Official Guide Book.   1s. 6d.

Trethevy Quoit, St. Cleer. (Pl. 2)

A prehistoric burial chamber consisting of five standing stones surmounted by a huge capstone.

Situation. 1 mile north-east of St. Cleer.

Railway Station. Liskeard.

Admission. At any time without charge.

SCILLY ISLES

Official Guide Book. All the monuments in the Isles of Scilly which are mentioned below are included in the guide to the Ancient Monuments of the Isles of Scilly, 1s. 6d.

St. Mary's, Bants Carn Burial Chamber and Ancient Village

A Bronze Age burial mound with entrance passage and chamber. Nearby are the remains of round and oval stone huts forming a village which was occupied in the middle of the Roman period.

Situation. 1 mile north of Hugh Town.

Railway Station. Penzance, thence by boat.

Admission. At any time without charge.

St. Mary's, Harry's Walls

A fort built in 1593 to command the harbour of St. Mary's Pool.

Situation. ¼ mile north-east of Hugh Town.

Railway Station. Penzance, thence by boat.

Admission. At any time without charge.

St. Mary's, Innisigden Burial Chamber

A small Bronze Age burial mound with well-built chamber.

Situation. 1¾ miles north-east of Hugh Town.

Railway Station. Penzance, thence by boat.

Admission. At any time without charge.

St. Mary's, Porth Hellick Down Burial Chamber

Probably the best preserved Bronze Age burial mound on the Islands, with entrance passage and chamber.

Situation. 1½ miles east of Hugh Town.

Railway Station. Penzance, thence by boat.

Admission. At any time without charge.

Tresco, King Charles's Castle

A castle probably built during the reign of Henry VIII for coast defence. Additional fortifications were built during the Civil War.

Situation. ¾ mile north-west of New Grimsby.

Railway Station. Penzance, thence by boat.

Admission. At any time without charge.

Tresco, Cromwell's Castle

A round tower built about the middle of the sixteenth century to house guns commanding the haven of New Grimsby. Alterations were made to it after the Civil War and again in the eighteenth century.

Situation. About 200 yards south-west of King Charles's Castle.

Railway Station. Penzance, thence by boat.

Admission. Exterior only, at any time without charge.

Tresco, The Old Blockhouse

Built towards the end of the sixteenth century as a battery for artillery.

Situation. On Block House Point, at the south end of Old Grimsby Harbour.

Railway Station. Penzance, thence by boat.

Admission. At any time without charge.

DEVONSHIRE

Blackbury Castle, Southleigh

An oval-shaped camp defended by a single bank and ditch with a complicated entrance on its southern side; probably of the Iron Age.

Situation. 1½ miles south-west of Southleigh.

Railway Station. Colyton.

Admission. At any time without charge.

*Dartmouth Castle. (Pl. 14)   25 - vi - '62

A small fifteenth-century fort, largely added to in the last quarter of the sixteenth century. It still had a Governor and was maintained in a fair state of repair until the middle of the last century.

Situation. 1½ miles south-east of Dartmouth.

Railway Station. Dartmouth.

Hours of Admission. Standard.

Admission Fee. 6d.

Official Guide Pamphlet. 2d.

*Lydford Castle

A twelfth-century keep with a rectangular bailey on its western side within the area of a Saxon burh. The castle was the seat of the Stannary Court until the court was moved to Princetown in the beginning of the last century.

Situation. In Lydford.

Railway Station. Lydford.

Admission. At any time without charge.

Official Guide Pamphlet. 2d.

Paignton, Kirkham House

A fourteenth-century stone house.

Situation. In Kirkham Street.

Railway Station. Paignton.

Admission. Not yet open to the public.

Plymouth, Citadel Gate

The Citadel is a large fortification erected after the Restoration. The elaborate entrance gateway is dated 1670.

Situation. To the east of Hoe Park.

Railway Station. Plymouth.

Admission. At any time without charge.

Plymouth, King George II's Statue

A statue representing George II in classical armour. It was erected by an officer of the garrison in 1728. During the war it was damaged by enemy action, and has been repaired by the Ministry of Works.

Situation. In the Citadel.

Railway Station. Plymouth.

Admission. At any time without charge, on application to the military authorities.

Totnes Castle

A large Norman motte and bailey castle, founded by Judhael in the time of the Conqueror. It was provided with a stone shell-keep and curtain wall in the twelfth century, which were reconstructed on the original pattern in the early fourteenth century. The keep is still remarkably complete.

Situation. On top of the hill, on the slopes of which the borough stands.

Railway Station. Totnes.

Hours of Admission. Standard.

Admission Fee. 3d.

Official Guide Pamphlet. 3d.

DORSETSHIRE

Abbotsbury, Abbey Buildings

The eastern gable of one of the conventual buildings of Abbotsbury Abbey.

Situation. In Abbotsbury, just south of the churchyard.

Railway Station. Abbotsbury.

Admission. At any time without charge.

Abbotsbury, St. Catherine's Chapel

A small fifteenth-century chapel with a fine decorated stone vault. Extensive views can be obtained from it in every direction and it was used as a beacon tower.

Situation. ½ mile south of Abbotsbury.

Railway Station. Abbotsbury.

Hours of Admission. At any time, on application at Town Farm, Abbotsbury.

Admission Fee. 3d.

Jordan Hill Roman Temple, Preston

Slight remains of a small rectangular Roman temple.

Situation. 2 miles north-east of Weymouth.

Railway Station. Weymouth.

Admission. At any time without charge.

Kingston Russell Stone Circle

A prehistoric circle of eighteen stones.

Situation. 2 miles north of Abbotsbury.

Railway Station. Abbotsbury.

Admission. At any time without charge.

**Maiden Castle, Dorchester.* (Pl. 4)

The finest known example of a prehistoric fortress in this country with enormous earthworks and complicated entrances. It dates from the Iron Age and superseded a neolithic camp. The remains of a fourth-century Roman temple have been discovered within the fortifications.

Situation. 2½ miles south-west of Dorchester.

Railway Station. Dorchester.

Admission. At any time without charge.

Official Guide Pamphlet. 4d.

The Nine Stones, Winterborne Abbas

Remains of a prehistoric stone circle consisting of nine standing stones.

Situation. South of the road about ½ mile west of Winterborne Abbas.

Railway Station. Dorchester.

Admission. At any time without charge.

Portland Castle

Erected by Henry VIII for coast defence and added to in the seventeenth century.

Situation. Overlooking Portland Harbour.

Railway Station. Portland.

Admission. Not yet open to the public.

Official Guide Book. In preparation.

HAMPSHIRE

Bishop's Waltham Palace 28 luno '64

Extensive ruins of a palace of the bishops of Winchester. The buildings are grouped about a rectangular courtyard enclosed by a moat, and include a keep built by Bishop Henry of Blois in the late twelfth century, and a great hall and lodgings added in the time of Bishop William of Wykeham.

Situation. In Bishop's Waltham.

Railway Station. Winchester, thence by bus.

Admission. Not yet open to the public.

Christchurch Norman House Sept '57

The first-floor hall of Christchurch Castle, built c. 1160. It retains some original windows and a Norman chimney.

Situation. In Christchurch.

Railway Station. Christchurch.

Admission. At all reasonable hours without charge.

Official Guide Book. In preparation.

*Hurst Castle 27 luno '64

Erected by Henry VIII for coast defence and added to in the seventeenth century, but now much altered.

Situation. 2½ miles south-east of Milford Church.

Railway Station. Lymington.

Hours of Admission. Standard.

Admission Fee. 3d.

Official Guide Pamphlet. 2d.

Netley Abbey. (Pl. 18)

Extensive and beautiful remains of a Cistercian abbey founded in 1239 by King Henry III. The walls of the greater part of the church and of the claustral buildings still stand, and there is much fine thirteenth-century architectural detail.

Situation. In Netley.

Railway Station. Netley.

Hours of Admission. Standard.

Admission Fee. 6d.

Official Guide Book, 1s.; *Pamphlet* 2d.

Portchester Castle. (Pl. 6) Sept '57

A large Roman fortress of the late third or early fourth century, of which practically the whole of the walls and bastions are standing. There is a mediæval castle in the north-west angle with a fine and practically perfect late Norman keep. The Norman church of an Augustinian Priory also stands within the Roman walls.

Situation. On the south side of Portchester.

Railway Station. Portchester.

Hours of Admission. Standard.

Admission Fee. 6d.

Official Guide Book, 1s.; *Pamphlet*, 2d.

Portsmouth, Garrison Church

This church was originally a hospital, founded by Bishop des Roches in 1214. The fine thirteenth-century chancel was the hospital chapel. The nave, which is modern, was badly damaged by enemy action during the war.

Situation. On Grand Parade to the south of High Street.

Railway Station. Portsmouth Harbour.

Admission. To the chancel, which is in use as the garrison church.

Portsmouth (a) King James's Gate
            (b) Landport Gate

Two gates of the defences of Portsmouth which were begun in 1665 by Charles II. The former was completed in 1687, the latter in 1698.

Situation. (a) Re-erected at the entrance to the Officers' recreation ground.

(b) In its original position, now forming the entrance to the Men's recreation ground.

Railway Station. Portsmouth Harbour.

Admission. Can be seen from the public streets.

*Titchfield Abbey.   (Pl. 16)

Founded as a house of Premonstratensian Canons in 1222, dissolved in 1537 and converted into a mansion by Thomas Wriothesley, Earl of Southampton. The south range and gate-house of the mansion which were incorporated in the nave of the monastic church are still practically complete. There are also remains of the chapter house and other monastic buildings.

Situation.   ½ mile north of Titchfield.

Railway Station.   Fareham.

Hours of Admission.   Standard.

Admission Fee.   6d.

Official Guide Pamphlet.   3d.

ISLE OF WIGHT

Appuldurcombe

The shell of a fine house, with Corinthian façades to the cardinal points. The building was begun by Sir Robert Worsley in 1710, close to the site of a cell of the Norman abbey of Montebourg. It was completed by Sir Richard Worsley who installed in it the celebrated Museum Worsleianum of paintings and classical antiquities commissioned and collected during a Grand Tour in 1785-7. The contents were later sold and the house became unoccupied in 1909.

Situation.   ½ mile west of Wroxall.

Railway Station.   Wroxall.

Admission.   Not yet open to the public.

*Carisbrooke Castle.   (Pl. 11)   Sept '57/

An extensive and important mediæval castle begun in the late eleventh century and considerably altered and added to later. Underlying the castle are the remains of a late Roman fort, the walls of which can be seen. King Charles I was imprisoned here. The Governor's Lodge houses the Isle of Wight County Museum.

Situation.   1¼ miles south-west of Newport.

Railway Station.   Newport, thence by bus.

Hours of Admission.   Standard hours on Weekdays and Sundays. Sundays, May to September, closed at 6 p.m.

Admission Fee.   1s.

Official Guide Book.   1s.

Niton, St. Catherine's Chapel

The west tower, used as a beacon, of a chapel of St. Catherine founded early in the fourteenth century as a result of the wreck of the wine-ship Ste. Marie of Bayonne.

Situation.   ¾ mile north-west of Niton.

Railway Station.   Ventnor.

Admission.   At any time without charge.

*Osborne House

Built as a private residence by Queen Victoria in 1845-6, with additions made during the second half of the nineteenth century. The Queen died here in 1901, having spent much of her married life and widowhood at the house.

The house is used as a Convalescent Home for Officers and is maintained by the Ministry of Works. The grounds, Queen Victoria's State Apartments, and the Swiss Cottage Museum are open to the public.

Situation. 1 mile south-east of Cowes.

Railway Station. Cowes.

Hours of Admission. Mondays, Wednesdays and Fridays, from 11.30 a.m. to 5 p.m., from Easter to the last Friday in September.

Admission Fee. 1s.

Official Guide Book. 1s. 6d.

Yarmouth Castle Sept '57

A small castle built by Henry VIII.

Situation. In Yarmouth.

Railway Station. Yarmouth.

Admission. A portion is open to the public without charge from 9 a.m. to 5.30 p.m.

KENT

*Canterbury, St. Augustine's Abbey 1946/ Sept '57/

Founded by St. Augustine on land given by King Ethelbert in 598. The foundations of the seventh-century church of Saints Peter and Paul, which was the burial place of the early archbishops and kings of Kent, and the remains of an eleventh-century round church underlie the extensive ruins of the mediæval Benedictine abbey.

Situation. In Canterbury.

Railway Station. Canterbury.

Hours of Admission. Standard.

Admission Fee. 6d.

Official Guide Book. In preparation.

*Canterbury, St. Pancras's Church

Founded by St. Augustine at the end of the sixth century. The nave and porticus are built of re-used Roman bricks. The chancel was reconstructed in the fourteenth century.

Situation. In Canterbury, east of St. Augustine's Abbey.

Railway Station. Canterbury.

Hours of Admission. Standard.

Admission Fee. Included in the admission to St. Augustine's Abbey

Deal Castle ~~XVI~~ - ~~IX~~ - ~~XVII~~

One of a series of castles built by Henry VIII for coast defence. It was damaged by enemy action during the war.

Situation. In Deal.

Railway Station. Deal.

Hours of Admission. Weekdays only, 2 p.m. to 8 p.m. No admission after 7 p.m. Closed during the winter months.

Admission Fee. 6*d.*

Official Guide Pamphlet. 6*d.*

*Dover Castle. (Pls. 9 and 10) ~~XVI~~ - ~~IX~~ - ~~XVII~~   *August 1946 , ___*

One of the largest and most important English castles dating from Norman times. The keep is surpassed in size only by those of London and Colchester. The great thickness of the walls, which at the base are 17 to 22 feet wide, permitted the construction of twenty-seven mural chambers within them, a number without parallel in any other English keep. In the fore-building are two ornate chapels of the late twelfth century. There is a fine thirteenth-century gate in the outer curtain wall. A Roman lighthouse and much restored Saxon church stand within the castle.

Situation. On the east side of Dover.

Railway Station. Dover.

Hours of Admission. Keep and underground passages, standard; grounds, standard on weekdays, Sunday hours as for weekdays.

Admission Fee. To the keep, 1*s.*; to the underground passages, 3*d.*; to the grounds, without charge.

Illustrated Guide. 1*s.* 6*d.*

Official Guide Pamphlet. 3*d.*

Dover, Knights Templars' Church

The foundations of a small circular twelfth-century church.

Situation. In the Citadel Barracks on the Western Heights above Dover.

Railway Station. Dover.

Admission. On application to the military authorities, without charge.

Ebbsfleet, St. Augustine's Cross

A modern cross marking the traditional site of the landing of St. Augustine in 597.

Situation. 2 miles east of Minster.

Railway Station. Minster.

Admission. At any time without charge.

Eynsford Castle   Maius ix ; VII Avrilus 'LXIII

A twelfth-century castle with remains of a high curtain wall and stone hall. - see End of book.

Situation.   In Eynsford.

Railway Station.   Eynsford.

Hours of Admission.   Standard.

Admission Fee.   6d.

Official Guide Book.   In preparation.

Horne's Place Chapel, Appledore   Sept '57

A fourteenth-century domestic chapel with undercroft, once attached to the manor house.

Situation.   1 mile north of Appledore. near Rye

Railway Station.   Appledore.

Admission.   Not yet open to the public.

(*a*) *Kit's Coty House, Aylesford*   Sept '57

The chamber of a prehistoric long barrow or burial place. The barrow originally consisted of a long earthen mound covering the chamber which contained the human remains.

(*b*) *Little Kit's Coty House, Aylesford*   Sept '57

A ruined burial chamber of a prehistoric long barrow.

Situation.   (*a*) On the west side of the Maidstone-Rochester road, $3\frac{1}{2}$ miles north of Maidstone.

(*b*) $\frac{1}{2}$ mile south of (*a*) on the east side of the Aylesford road.

Railway Station.   Aylesford.

Admission.   At any time without charge.

Lullingstone Roman Villa; VII Avrilus 'LXIII

Old Soar Manor, Plaxtol   XIII - IX - 'LVII

A fine example of a thirteenth-century house, with solar over vaulted undercroft, and chapel. The hall has been replaced by an eighteenth-century farm-house. National Trust property, placed in the guardianship of the Ministry of Works.

Situation.   About 6 miles north-north-east of Tonbridge and 1 mile east of Plaxtol village.

Railway Station.   Wrotham.

Hours of Admission.   Standard.

Admission Fee.   6d.

Official Guide Pamphlet.   3d.

Ospringe, Maison Dieu

A fifteenth-century timber-framed building on the site of a hospital founded by Henry III. It contains pottery from the Roman cemetery at Ospringe.

Situation. In Ospringe village, ½ mile west of Faversham.

Railway Station. Faversham.

Admission. Not yet open to the public.

*Reculver Towers and Roman Fort   Mars' LXII

The remains of a Saxon church founded in the seventh century standing within the walls of a Roman fortress. The early church was altered and enlarged during the Middle Ages and the towers are of late twelfth-century date.

Situation. At Reculver, 3 miles east of Herne Bay.

Railway Station. Herne Bay.

Hours of Admission. Standard.

Admission Fee. To the church 3*d.* To the Roman fort at any time without charge.

Official Guide Pamphlet. 2*d.*

Richborough Amphitheatre   XVI - IX - LVII

An amphitheatre serving the Roman fort at Richborough, and measuring 200 ft. by 166 ft. Not yet excavated.

Situation. ¼ mile south-west of Richborough Castle.

Railway Station. Sandwich.

Admission. At any time without charge.

*Richborough Castle.   (Pl. 5)   XVI - IX - LVII

The Roman invading army landed here in A.D. 43 and a stretch of earthworks then thrown up can be seen. The site became a military supply depot during the advance of the victorious armies, and later a commercial town and one of the principal ports of Roman Britain. In the late third century a fort was built here and its massive walls still stand to a height of 25 feet. Towards the end of the first century a large monument cased with Italian marble was erected, probably to commemorate the conquest of Britain, while in Saxon times a chapel to St. Augustine, who is reputed to have landed here, was built within the walls.

Situation. 1½ miles north of Sandwich.

Railway Station. Sandwich.

Hours of Admission. Standard.

Admission Fee. 6*d.*

Official Guide Pamphlet. 3*d.*

Rochester, Temple Manor

The thirteenth-century hall, with vaulted undercroft, of a manor house of the Knights Templar. Extensive sixteenth- and seventeenth-century additions have mostly been demolished.

Situation. On the west bank of the Medway, $\frac{1}{2}$ mile south-west of Rochester Bridge.

Railway Station. Strood.

Admission. Not yet open to the public.

*Walmer Castle   XVI - IX - XVII

One of the series of castles for coast defence built by Henry VIII. The castle is the residence of the Lord Warden of the Cinque Ports. The rooms occupied by the Duke of Wellington, who spent his last days here, still contain his furniture and have been preserved unaltered.

Situation. South of Walmer.

Railway Station. Walmer.

Hours of Admission. Weekdays, standard; closed on Sundays. The gardens are closed during the winter months.

Admission Fee. To castle and gardens, 1s. Gardens only, 3d. (no party rates).

Official Guide Pamphlet. 2d.

West Malling, St. Leonard's Tower 12·4·63

A fine early Norman tower built by Gundulf, Bishop of Rochester.

Situation. $\frac{1}{4}$ mile south-west of West Malling.   Late 11ᵗʰ C. - two

Railway Station. West Malling.   storey - good state of

Admission. At any time without charge, on application to the caretaker. preservation.

12·4·63 Upnor Castle: Elizabethan fort or bastion protecting Rochester.

LONDON (South of Thames)

*Greenwich Royal Naval College

The Royal Naval College occupied the buildings of the Hospital founded in 1694 for disabled seamen of the Royal Navy. The Painted Hall, designed by Wren and completed by Vanbrugh as a Dining Hall, was decorated by Thornhill between 1708 and 1727 with allegorical paintings. The chapel, which was burnt in 1797, was restored by the architect James Stuart.

* On sale at the Queen's House, Greenwich, only.

Situation. On Thames-side at Greenwich.

Railway Station. Maze Hill or Greenwich.

Hours of Admission. Weekdays 2.30 p.m. to 5 p.m.; Sundays, June to September, 2.30 p.m. to 5 p.m. Closed on Thursdays.

Admission Fee. No charge.

Greenwich Royal Observatory

Flamsteed House was built in 1675-6 under a Royal Warrant of 1675 establishing a Royal Observatory for "the finding out the longitude of places for perfecting navigation and astronomy". Its site was formerly occupied by Greenwich Castle, a tower built by Humphrey, Duke of Gloucester, and repaired or rebuilt by Henry VIII in 1526. Sir Christopher Wren was in charge of the work and the Reverend John Flamsteed, after whom the house is now called, was the first Astronomer Royal. A stone mark, north of the building, marks the position of the zero meridian of longitude.

Situation. In Greenwich Park.

Railway Stations. Maze Hill or Greenwich.

Admission. Not yet open to the public.

Queen's House, Greenwich. (Pl. 20)

This house was designed by Inigo Jones and completed in 1635 and is an outstanding example of his work. It was enlarged in 1662. Additions made in the early nineteenth century, when the house was granted to the Greenwich Hospital School, have been removed; much of the original decoration has been exposed. It now contains part of the collection of the National Maritime Museum.

Situation. On the north side of Greenwich Park.

Railway Station. Maze Hill.

Hours of Admission. Weekdays, 10 a.m. to 6 p.m.; Sundays, 2.30 p.m. to 6 p.m. In winter the house is closed at dusk.

Admission Fee. No charge.

SOMERSET

Cleeve Abbey 7 Maius-65

A Cistercian abbey founded by William de Roumara, Earl of Lincoln, towards the end of the twelfth century. Only the foundations of the church remain, but the greater part of the claustral buildings survives almost intact and includes the frater with a fine timber roof. The gatehouse was built by the last abbot.

Situation. At the south end of Washford village.

Railway Station. Washford.

Hours of Admission. Standard.

Admission Fee. 1s.

Official Guide Book. In preparation.

Dunster, Butter Cross 8 Maius-65

A stone cross, said to have been moved from Dunster High Street. Also known as Rockhead Cross. Very worn pillar

Situation. Beside the road to Alcombe, 400 yards north-west of Dunster Parish Church.

Railway Station. Dunster.

Admission. At any time without charge.

Dunster, Gallox Bridge 8 - Maius - 65

A stone packhorse bridge with two ribbed arches, in picturesque surroundings.

Situation. At the southern end of Dunster.

Railway Station. Dunster.

Admission. At any time without charge.

Dunster, Yarn Market 8 - Maius 65

An octagonal market hall, built by the Luttrells of Dunster Castle in 1609 and repaired in 1647. It was used for the sale of cloth woven locally.

Situation. In the High Street.

Railway Station. Dunster.

Admission. At any time without charge.

*Farleigh Castle xi Maius '63

Dates from the late fourteenth century and consists of two courts defended by walls and towers. In the outer court is the chapel, formerly the parish church, containing a fine tomb of Sir Thomas Hungerford, the builder of the castle. and also a fine museum armour etc.

Situation. In Farleigh Hungerford, 3½ miles west of Trowbridge (Wilts.).

Railway Station. Trowbridge.

Hours of Admission. Standard.

Admission Fee. 6d.

Official Guide Pamphlet. 2d.

*Glastonbury Tribunal 29 Iuno '62

The fifteenth-century courthouse of Glastonbury Abbey, re-fronted by Abbot Bere between 1493 and 1524.

Situation. In High Street, Glastonbury.

Railway Station. Glastonbury.

Hours of Admission. Standard.

Admission Fee. 3d.

Official Guide Pamphlet. 3d.

Meare, Abbot's Fish House

A fourteenth-century building used in connection with the fishery of Glastonbury Abbey.

Situation. At the eastern end of Meare village.

Railway Station. Ashcott.

Admission. At any time without charge.

Plate 17. Muchelney Abbey

Plate 18.   NETLEY ABBEY

Plate 19. OLD WARDOUR CASTLE

Plate 20. Greenwich, the Queen's House

*Muchelney Abbey. (Pl. 17)

Part of the claustral buildings of this mediæval Benedictine abbey still stand in a very complete state. They consist of the south walk of the cloister, part of the frater, the kitchen and the Abbot's lodging. There is some fine detail of the fifteenth and early sixteenth centuries. Excavations have revealed the plan of the Abbey Church and of the pre-conquest church that was its predecessor.

Situation. In Muchelney, 2 miles south of Langport.

Railway Station. Langport East.

Hours of Admission. Standard.

Admission Fee. 6d.

Official Guide Book. In preparation.

*Nunney Castle. (Pl. 13) Mont. 21/uno '45

A small but very complete and interesting castle of late fourteenth-century date standing in a moat. It is rectangular with large round towers at the angles. It was bombarded by the Parliamentarians in 1645, the castle falling on the second day of the siege.

Situation. In Nunney, about 3½ miles south-west of Frome.

Railway Station. Frome.

Hours of Admission. Standard.

Admission Fee. 3d. free

Official Guide Pamphlet. 3d. ?

Stanton Drew Circles and Cove

Three prehistoric stone circles, the remains of two avenues of standing stones and a prehistoric burial chamber. One of the finest monuments of this description in the country, and probably of the same date as Avebury.

Situation. Circles, to the east of the village of Stanton Drew. The Cove, in the garden of the Druid's Arms.

Railway Station. Pensford.

Hours of Admission. At any time.

Admission Fee. To the Circles, 3d. To the Cove, 3d.

Stoney Littleton Long Barrow

A prehistoric burial place consisting of a long passage with recesses on both sides where the human remains were deposited. The walls of the passage and recesses are of dry-built masonry roofed with large slabs of stone, the whole being covered with an earthen mound. A tablet on the monument records its restoration in 1858.

Situation. 1 mile south of Wellow.

Railway Station. Wellow.

Admission. On application at Stoney Littleton Farm.

Admission Fee. 3d.

74

NOTES

Weston, Sir Bevil Granville's Monument XI Maius '63

An early eighteenth century monument to Sir Bevil Granville, slain at the battle of Lansdown, 1643.

Situation. On Lansdown Hill, near road to Wick, 4 miles north-west of Bath.

Railway Station. Bath.

Admission. At any time, without charge.

SURREY

*Farnham Castle 28 Iuno '64

Dates from the eleventh century onwards and was occupied by the Bishops of Winchester. An important military centre in the Middle Ages and the scene of fighting in the early part of the Civil War. The twelfth-century shell keep which stands on an earlier mound is open to the public.

Situation. In Farnham.

Railway Station. Farnham.

Hours of Admission. Standard.

Admission Fee. 3d.

Un-official Guide Book on sale.

Ham House, Petersham

Begun c. 1610, this famous early seventeenth-century house was enlarged after the Restoration when it was the residence of the Duke of Lauderdale. Its almost unrivalled contemporary furnishings are in the care of the Victoria and Albert Museum. The house is National Trust property and is maintained by the Ministry of Works.

Situation. In Petersham, 1½ miles south of Richmond.

Railway Station. Richmond.

Hours of Admission. Saturdays and Bank Holidays 10 a.m.-6 p.m. (Winter 10 a.m.-4 p.m.); Sundays 2.30 p.m.-6 p.m. (winter 2.30 p.m.-4 p.m.); from Monday to Friday the public are taken round only in guided parties at 10.30 a.m., 11.30 a.m., 2.30 p.m. and 3.30 p.m.

Admission Fee. To the house, 1s. To the grounds without charge.

Official Guide Book. 1s. 6d.

Kew Palace

An early seventeenth-century house built for a London merchant. Bought by King George III in 1781 and was the residence of royalty until the death of Queen Charlotte in 1818.

Situation. Inside the Royal Botanical Gardens, Kew.

Railway Station. Kew Gardens (Midland Region and Underground).

Hours of Admission. 11 a.m. to 6 p.m.; Sundays, 1 p.m. to 6 p.m.

Admission Fee. 1s. (in addition to the entrance fee to the Gardens).

SUSSEX

Pevensey Castle. (Pl. 7) *August '46 & xiv - ix - xvii*

Extensive remains of a large Roman fortress of the late third century. A castle dating from the late eleventh century was built in the eastern end of the Roman fortress and there are considerable remains of the keep, the thirteenth-century curtain walls, towers and gatehouse.

Situation. In Pevensey.

Railway Station. Pevensey.

Hours of Admission. Standard.

Admission Fee. 6d.

Official Guide Book, 1s.; *Pamphlet*, 3d.

WILTSHIRE

Avebury. (Pl. 1)

A complex megalithic monument of c. 1900-1800 B.C., originally consisting of two or perhaps three stone circles. Later in the same period, an outer stone circle and bank and ditch were constructed. Many stones were destroyed or cast down in the seventeenth and eighteenth centuries; some have been re-erected and the sites of others marked with concrete blocks. The West Kennett Avenue of standing stones (some re-erected) runs southwards to the Sanctuary, Overton Hill (see below). National Trust property in the guardianship of the Ministry of Works.

Situation. 7 miles west of Marlborough.

Railway Station. Marlborough, thence by bus.

Hours of Admission. To the Museum, standard. To the site, at any time without charge.

Admission Fee. To the Museum, 6d.

Unofficial Guide Pamphlet. 1s.

Bradford-on-Avon Tithe Barn ×1 *Maius '63*

A fine fourteenth-century barn which belonged to Shaftesbury Abbey.

Situation. At Barton Farm, ¼ mile south-west of Bradford-on-Avon.

Railway Station. Bradford-on-Avon.

Hours of Admission. At any time.

Admission Fee. ~~3d.~~ Free

Unofficial Guide Pamphlet. 2d.

Bratton Camp and White Horse, Westbury

A large prehistoric camp probably of the Iron Age with a long barrow of earlier date within the fortifications. The White Horse cut in the turf below the camp is in its present form of eighteenth-century date.

Situation. 1 mile south-west of Bratton and 2 miles east of Westbury.

Railway Station. Westbury.

Admission. At any time without charge.

Ludgershall Castle and Cross

All that now exists of this Norman castle is extensive earthworks and some fragments of buildings. The Village Cross, in the main street, is also in the Ministry's charge.

Situation. On the north side of Ludgershall.

Railway Station. Ludgershall.

Admission. At any time without charge.

Netheravon Dovecot

An eighteenth-century brick dovecot retaining most of its chalk nesting-boxes.

Situation. In Netheravon, $4\frac{1}{2}$ miles north of Amesbury.

Railway Station. Amesbury, thence by bus.

Admission. At any time without charge, on application at Netheravon House.

*Old Sarum. (Pl. 8)

Probably originally an Iron Age hill-fort, then a Saxon burh, and Norman town. The enormous and extensive earthworks are of late eleventh-century date. Excavation has revealed extensive remains of the castle and cathedral. The latter was moved to Salisbury between 1220 and 1230. A small museum containing architectural fragments is on the site.

Situation. 2 miles north of Salisbury.

Railway Station. Salisbury.

Hours of Admission. Standard

Admission Fee. 6d.

Official Guide Pamphlet. 6d.

*Old Wardour Castle. (Pl. 19)

A hexagonal castle surrounding a central courtyard, built by John, Lord Lovel, in 1392, with alterations in the Renaissance style added after 1570. The west side was blown up during the siege in the Civil War.

Situation. In Wardour Park, 2 miles south-west of Tisbury.

Railway Station. Tisbury.

Admission Fee. 6d.

Official Guide Book. In preparation.

The Sanctuary, Overton Hill

The West Kennett Avenue of standing stones connected this monument with Avebury. The sanctuary consisted of two concentric circles of stones and six of timber uprights, the sites of which are marked by low concrete pillars. It was probably erected in the Early Bronze Age.

Situation. Beside the Bath Road, $\frac{1}{2}$ mile east of the village of West Kennett.

Railway Station. Marlborough.

Admission. At any time without charge.

Silbury Hill, Avebury

An artificial prehistoric mound, the largest existing example of this type in Europe. Believed to be sepulchral, and probably dating from Early Bronze Age.

Situation. Beside the Bath Road, 1 mile west of the village of West Kennett.

Railway Station. Marlborough.

Admission. At any time without charge.

*Stonehenge. (Pl. 3)

A prehistoric monument of world-wide fame, consisting of a series of stone circles, one within another, all being surrounded by a ditch and approached by an "avenue" on the east side. It may be assigned to the period between 1800 and 1500 B.C.

Situation. 2 miles west of Amesbury.

Railway Station. Amesbury.

Hours of Admission. Standard; also open during standard weekday hours on Sunday mornings from March to September.

Admission Fee. 6d.

Official Guide Book. 1s. 6d.

Official Guide Pamphlet. 2d.

West Kennett Long Barrow

A prehistoric burial place near Avebury consisting of a long earthen mound containing a chamber, formed of large blocks of stone, in which the human remains were placed.

Situation. ¾ mile south-west of the village of West Kennett.

Railway Station. Marlborough.

Admission. At any time without charge.

Windmill Hill

A neolithic circular earthwork, excavated about twenty years ago. The finds then made are in Avebury Museum. National Trust property in the guardianship of the Ministry of Works.

Situation. 1 mile north of Avebury.

Railway Station. Marlborough, thence by bus.

Admission. At any time without charge.

Woodhenge, Durrington

This monument consisted of six concentric rings of timber posts surrounded by a ditch with a bank on the outside. It was entered by a causeway on the north-west. The rings are oval, the long axis pointing to the rising sun on Midsummer Day. The burial of a child was found in the centre. The positions of the posts are marked with low concrete pillars.

Situation. Beside the Pewsey road, 2 miles north of Amesbury.

Railway Station. Amesbury.

Admission. At any time without charge.

BIBLIOGRAPHY

Generally

THE VICTORIA COUNTY HISTORIES.
THE COUNTY ARCHÆOLOGIES:—
    Berkshire. Peake, H. 1931.
    Cornwall. Hencken, H. O'N. 1932.
    Kent. Jessup, R. F. 1930.
    Somerset. Dobson, D. P. 1931.
    Surrey. Whimster, D. C. 1931.
KENDRICK, T. D., and HAWKES, C. F. C. Archæology in England and Wales (1914-1931). 1932.
CRAWFORD, O. G. S., and KEILLER, A. Wessex from the Air. 1928.

Prehistoric Period

CHILDE, V. G. Prehistoric Communities of the British Isles.
CLARK, GRAHAME. Prehistoric England.
CURWEN, E. C. Prehistoric Sussex. 1930.
FOX, Sir CYRIL. Personality of Britain.
HAWKES, C. F. C. and J. J. Prehistoric Britain. 1947.
ORDNANCE SURVEY OFFICE:—
    Field Archæology. 1932.
    Map of Neolithic Wessex. 1932.
PIGGOTT, S. British Prehistory. 1949.
QUENNELL, M. and C. Everyday Life in Prehistoric Times. 1924.
WHEELER, R. E. M. Maiden Castle, Dorset. 1943.

Roman Period

BUSHE-FOX, J. P. Excavations at Richborough.
COLLINGWOOD, R. C. The Archæology of Roman Britain. 1930.
HAVERFIELD. Romanisation of Roman Britain. 1907.
MOTHERSOLE, J. The Saxon Shore. 1924.
ORDNANCE SURVEY OFFICE. Map of Roman Britain. 1934.
QUENNELL, M. and C. Everyday Life in Roman Britain. 1924.

Anglo-Saxon Period

BROWN, G. BALDWIN. The Arts in Early England. 1903-34.
HODGKIN, R. H. History of the Anglo-Saxons. 1935.
LEEDS, E. T. Archæology of the Anglo-Saxon Settlements. 1913.
ORDNANCE SURVEY OFFICE. Map of the Dark Ages. 1935.
QUENNELL, M. and C. Everyday Life in Anglo-Saxon, Viking, and Norman Times. 1926.

Monastic Buildings

CLAPHAM, A. W.
    English Romanesque Architecture before the Conquest. 1930.
    English Romanesque Architecture after the Conquest. 1934.

CRANAGE, D. H. S. The Home of the Monk. 1926.

GASQUET, F. A. English Monastic Life. 1904.

JAMES, M. R. Abbeys. 1926.

THOMPSON, A. H. English Monasteries. 1923.

Castles

ARMITAGE, E. S. Early Norman Castles. 1912.

BURROWS, M. The Cinque Ports. 1903.

O'NEIL, B. H. St. J. Castles. 1953.

THOMPSON, A. H. Military Architecture in England during the Middle Ages. 1912.

INDEX

Page

Abbotsbury Abbey ... 38-39, 62
Abingdon County Hall ... 55
Appuldurcombe 65
Avebury ... 10, 12, 14, 15, 24, 25, 75

Bants Carn burial chamber 13, 59
Bath 27
Berwick-on-Tweed 49
Bewcastle 34
Bignor Roman villa 27
Bishop's Waltham Palace ... 63
Blackbury Castle ... 21, 60
Bokerley Dyke 31-32
Bradford-on-Avon tithe barn 39, 75
Brading Roman villa 27
Bratton Camp, Westbury 20, 23, 75

Camber Castle 48
Canterbury 26, 27, 32
Carisbrooke Castle 29, 37, 43-44, 46,
49, 65
Chichester 26, 27
Christchurch 35
Christchurch Norman house 50, 63
Chysauster ancient village 21, 56
Cissbury Ring 19
Cleeve Abbey 36-37, 71
Colchester 26, 41
Cranborne Chase ... 18, 32
Cromwell's Castle ... 49, 60

Dartmouth Castle ... 48, 60
Deal Castle 49, 67
Donnington Castle 56
Dorchester 26, 27
Dover 27, 29, 42
Dover Castle 41-42, 67
Dunster Butter Cross 71
Dunster Yarn Market 72
Dupath Well Chapel ... 39, 56

Exeter 26, 27
Eynsford Castle 43, 68

Farleigh Castle 47, 72
Farnham Castle 44, 74
Faversham 32
Folkestone Roman villa ... 27

Page

Flint Castle 46

Gallox Bridge, Dunster ... 72
Glastonbury 21
Glastonbury Abbey 38
Glastonbury Tribunal ... 34, 38, 72
Gloucester 27
Greenwich Royal Naval College 70
Greenwich Royal Observatory 71
Grime's Graves 12

Ham Hill Camp 20
Ham House 53, 54, 74
Hampton Court 37
Harlyn Bay 13
Harry's Walls 50, 59
Hembury Camp 20
Hod Hill Camp 26
Horne's Place Chapel ... 39, 68
Hurlers, stone circles ... 17, 57
Hurst Castle 49, 63

Icknield Way 12
Innisigden burial chamber 13, 59

Jordan Hill Roman temple 29, 62

Kew Palace 53, 74
King Charles's Castle ... 49, 60
King Doniert's inscribed stone
34-35, 57
Kingston Russell stone circle 17, 62
Kirkham House, Paignton 51, 61
Kit's Coty House ... 10, 68
Knights Templars' Church,
Dover 39, 67

Launceston Castle ... 46, 57
Little Kit's Coty House 10, 68
Ludgershall Castle ... 44-45, 76
Lydford Castle 45, 61
Lydney 30
Lympne 27

Maiden Castle 10, 20-21, 26, 29-30,
62

Page

Malmesbury 35
Meare, Abbot's Fish House 38, 72
Meare Lake Village 21
Muchelney Abbey 34, 36, 39, 73

Netheravon dovecot 76
Netley Abbey 37, 64
Nine Stones, Winterborne
  Abbas 17, 63
Niton, St. Catherine's Chapel ... 65
Nunney Castle 47, 73

Oakley Down Roman road ... 27
Old Blockhouse, Tresco 50, 60
Old Sarum 40-41, 76
Old Soar Manor House 51, 68
Old Wardour Castle ... 47-48, 76
Osborne House 66
Ospringe Maison Dieu 51, 69

Pendennis Castle ... 48-50, 57
Pevensey Castle 28-29, 42, 75
Plymouth Citadel Gate 54, 61
Plymouth, King George II's
  statue 61
Portchester Castle 27-29, 35, 42, 64
Porth Hellick Down burial
  chamber 13, 59
Portland Castle 49, 63
Portsmouth Garrison Church 39, 64
Portsmouth, King James's Gate 54,
  64
Portsmouth, Landport Gate 54, 64

Queen's House, Greenwich 51-53,
  71

Reculver Church and Roman
  fort 27-28, 33-34, 69
Restormel Castle ... 45, 58
Richborough Amphitheatre ... 69
Richborough Castle 25-28, 34, 69
Ruthwell 34

St. Alban's 23
St. Augustine's Abbey, Canterbury 33, 35-36, 66
St. Augustine's Cross, Ebbsfleet 67

Page

St. Breock Downs, monolith 58
St. Catherine's Castle, Fowey 48, 58
St. Catherine's Chapel, Abbots-
  bury 38-39, 62
St. Leonard's Tower, West
  Malling 42-43, 70
St. Martin's Church, Canter-
  bury 32
St. Mary-in-Castro, Dover 29, 35
St. Mawe's Castle ... 48, 58
St. Pancras's Church, Canter-
  bury 33, 66
Sanctuary, West Kennett 14-15, 76
Sherborne 35
Silbury Hill 15, 77
Silchester 23, 26
Stanton Drew Circles and Cove
  12, 14, 17, 73
Stonehenge ... 12, 14, 16, 25, 77
Stoney Littleton long barrow
  10-11, 73

Temple Manor, Rochester 39, 70
Tilbury Fort 54
Tintagel Castle ... 31, 35, 45-46, 58
Titchfield Abbey ... 37-38, 65
Totnes Castle 46, 61
Tower of London ... 41, 43
Trethevy Quoit ... 10, 13, 59
Trundle, The 19

Uffington Castle ... 20, 56

Walmer Castle 42, 49, 70
Wansdyke 31-32
Watling Street 27
Wayland's Smithy ... 10, 56
West Kennett long barrow 10, 15, 77
Weston, Sir Bevil Granville's
  Monument 74
White Horse, Uffington 20, 22, 23,
  56
White Horse, Westbury 23, 75
Winchester 26, 27, 44
Windmill Hill 10, 15, 77
Woodhenge 16-17, 77

Yarmouth Castle ... 49, 66

Printed in Great Britain under the authority of Her Majesty's Stationery Office
by Joseph Wones Ltd., West Bromwich

(2418) Wt. 3337/L1903 K24 9/54 J.W.Ltd. Gp. 517   S.O. Code No. 67-9-2*

Eynsford Castle - Kent:

12:C. curtain wall - roughly oval, of flint
it's wall walk must have been it's only
defence as no towers intervening & no
gatehouse as original entrance was high
in N. wall. Walls were probably 30' high
& 6' thick; no wall walk left intact &
W. side has collapsed in tote. While surrounded
by wide & deep moat (now dry) fed by
River Darent.

Little remains of rectangular shaped
keep at North end of enclosure (30' × 40')
Was probably three floors height (-ie-
including ground floor)

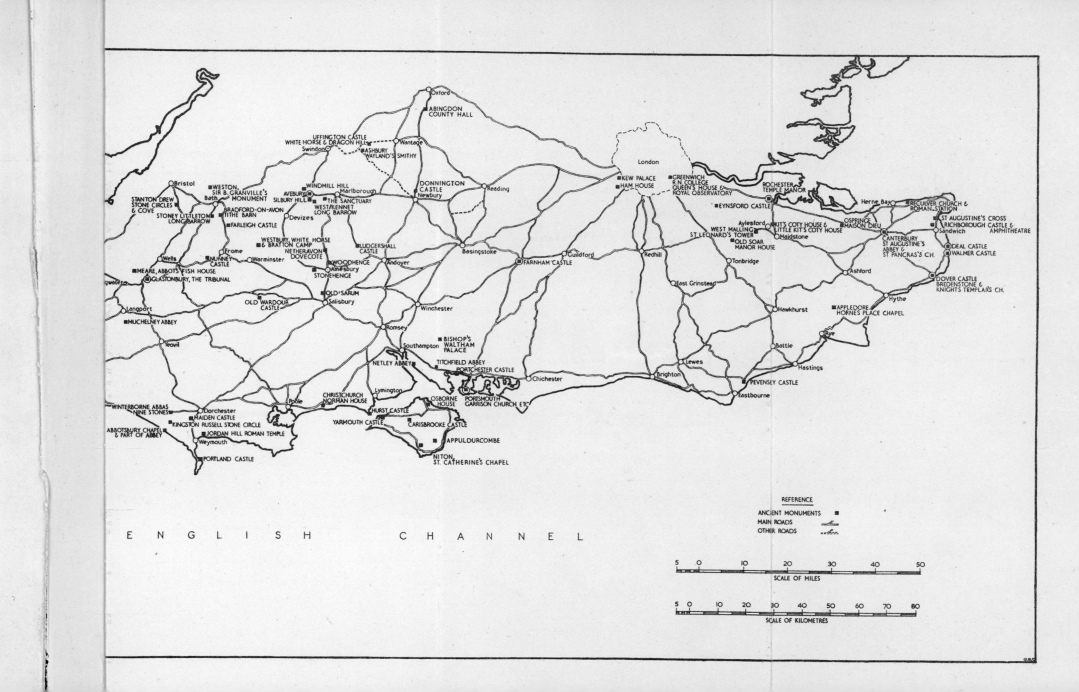

REFERENCE

ANCIENT MONUMENTS ■
MAIN ROADS
OTHER ROADS

SCALE OF MILES
5 0 10 20 30 40 50

SCALE OF KILOMETRES
5 0 10 20 30 40 50 60 70 80

ENGLISH   CHANNEL